# HIP HOP'S LI'L SISTAS SPEAK

# Studies in the Postmodern Theory of Education

Shirley R. Steinberg
*General Editor*

Vol. 399

The Counterpoints series is part of the Peter Lang Education list.
Every volume is peer reviewed and meets
the highest quality standards for content and production.

PETER LANG
New York • Washington, D.C./Baltimore • Bern
Frankfurt • Berlin • Brussels • Vienna • Oxford

BETTINA L. LOVE

# HIP HOP'S LI'L SISTAS SPEAK

## NEGOTIATING HIP HOP IDENTITIES AND POLITICS IN THE NEW SOUTH

PETER LANG
New York • Washington, D.C./Baltimore • Bern
Frankfurt • Berlin • Brussels • Vienna • Oxford

**Library of Congress Cataloging-in-Publication Data**

Love, Bettina L.
Hip hop's li'l sistas speak: negotiating hip hop identities and politics
in the new South / Bettina L. Love.
p. cm. — (Counterpoints: studies in the postmodern theory of education; v. 399)
Includes bibliographical references and index.
1. Hip-hop feminism—Georgia—Atlanta—Case studies. 2. African American teenage girls—Georgia—Atlanta—Case studies. 3. Hip-hop—Influence—Case studies. 4. Sexism in music—Case studies. 5. Music and teenagers—Georgia—Atlanta—Case studies. 6. Music—Social aspects—Georgia—Atlanta—Case studies. 7. Women—Identity—Case studies. 8. African Americans—Race identity—Case studies. 9. African Americans—Education—Social aspects—Case studies. I. Title.
HQ1421.L68 305.309758—dc23 2012036411
ISBN 978-1-4331-1191-4 (hardcover)
ISBN 978-1-4331-1190-7 (paperback)
ISBN 978-1-4539-0925-6 (e-book)
ISSN 1058-1634

Bibliographic information published by **Die Deutsche Nationalbibliothek**.
**Die Deutsche Nationalbibliothek** lists this publication in the "Deutsche Nationalbibliografie"; detailed bibliographic data is available on the Internet at http://dnb.d-nb.de/.

Cover Art: John Jennings
Book Design & Photography: Tiffany Stubbs

The paper in this book meets the guidelines for permanence and durability of the Committee on Production Guidelines for Book Longevity of the Council of Library Resources.

29 Broadway, 18th floor, New York, NY 10006
www.peterlang.com



Printed in the United States of America

"This soil is bad for certain kinds of flowers."
— Toni Morrison, *The Bluest Eye*

# Contents

# Acknowledgments

This book, my work, and my drive are because of God; my family; Rochester, New York; and Hip Hop music and culture. I am thankful that the Creator sees something in me and allows me to follow my dream. There are so many people to thank, but first I have to thank a place: Rochester, New York. I could not have been nurtured in a better place. I owe my life and wit to the guys on the street corners who made sure I got home safe at night, taught me how to play basketball, and always treated me with the upmost respect. I love you all. I am a stronger woman today because of you. I extend gratitude to all the coaches (Eddie Lee, Nally, Karl, Tony, Mario, and Fat Daddy [Gregory Bodine]) who taught me how to play basketball and created a community that never stopped believing in me. To Karen, director of Flint St. Recreation Center, and Ms. James, director of the Boys & Girls Club, I am inspired by your commitment to inner-city kids. You were some of my first female role models. Thank you for always pushing me toward my goals before I even knew I had goals. To my parents, I thank you for your unconditional love and for allowing me the space to be myself. This book would not have been possible without my love for music that my mother (Patty) and my father (Love) initiated at an early age, which was then cultivated by my brother. Patty, you exemplify strength. I learned how to be strong and resourceful from you. Gene, I love you for always being a big brother. To my sister, thank you for your love and commitment to my academic success, even before I ever picked up a book. My grandmother never learned how to read, but she taught me that common sense and confidence are no less important than a book—thank you, Grandma Rose.

Mrs. Knight, you have worn many hats in my life—athletic director, mentor, academic advisor, and, most significantly, mother; thank you for your guidance and unmovable belief in me. Thank you, Mr. Knight, for embracing me as your daughter as well. To the Nally family, your support has been amazing. Mary Beth and Coach, you believed in me before I knew that I could play basketball and compete on a collegiate level. Your confidence in me was the impetus for me to believe in myself. I could never have left Rochester without these two amazing families—the Nallys and the Knights. Coach and Mrs. Knight, thank you for always seeing more in me than just a basketball player. Drina and Tina, high school was just the start to a life-long sisterhood that I cherish every day.

I have never met two women so strong, giving, and supportive. I love you two, not as my friends, but as my sisters. Zook, thank you for teaching me how to be a fearless ball player. Ms. Betty, thank you for every night you let me sleep on your couch and never asked a single question. Myles, you are the best nephew an aunt could have. I love every second I get to spend with you, and I am proud of all your accomplishments. You motivate me to be the best role model I can be—thank you. Tom and Lydia, thank you for your support and words of encouragement; they were more than words to me. Elita and Ms. Bradley, thank you for your support and love during this process. I thank the Gunter and Stubbs family, Brandelyn and Bruce Tosolt, and Earl and Shenese Lewis for their support and love.

I have to thank Dr. Russell Irvine and Dr. Asa Hilliard for being my first academic mentors and inspiring me to fight for all people through knowledge. My work could never reflect the impact these two men have had on my life and my research. Dr. Esposito, your support and friendship over the years has meant a lot to me. I have grown so much as a scholar because of you. Thank you for believing in me and challenging my ideas. Cutts and Corrie, your friendship, love, and candid feedback are a few of the major reasons I completed my dissertation and now have the ability to turn it into a book. I thank you for your support and friendship. I am fortunate to have your friendship and strength supporting me. Lara Say and Rahna Carusi, I cannot say thank you enough for all your edits and feedback. Also, a big thank you to Derrick Alridge, Andreana Clay, and Greg Dimitriadis for reading particular chapters of the book and providing invaluable input, which has made me a better writer and thinker. I am a fan of the work of all three of you, so to have your feedback on my first book is mind-blowing. However, any shortcomings in the book are my own. To my new colleagues at UGA, thank you for supporting my work and creating such a caring and scholarly space.

To my editor, Shirley Steinberg, you are a true social justice scholar who walks the walk and talks the talk. I admire your candor, which is laced with intellectual rigor. I cannot say thank you enough for trusting me with a book in your series and believing in my work. Big thank you to John Jennings for creating such a dope book cover. I am honored to have a piece of your work attached to mine. To the hardworking, dedicated, and patient folks at Peter Lang, thank you. Tiffany Stubbs, thank you for lending me your creative mind and energy for this project; I could not have designed this book without you.

To my wife, Chelsey, thank you. However, the phrase "thank you" does not begin to capture the gratitude I want to express. This book is our book. All the late nights, all the frustration, and all the days when I thought I would never finish, you were there encouraging me and believing in my vision. I can never repay you or say thank you enough for your love, support, and belief in me. Chelsey, thank you for your sacrifice, patience, and unconditional love for my dream, which I know is our dream. I love you. To my babies, Chance and Lauryn, "nothing even matters."

Lastly, to the youth of Hope Community Center (HCC), THANK YOU for sharing your dreams and fears with me. You made me a better researcher, educator, and woman. To the staff of HCC, I thank you for extending your center and time to me. I will never forget the dreams of the youth at HCC and how their words shaped me.

Peace!

# Permissions

One of the chapters in this book appeared previously in the following publication:

Chapter 5 was taken from Love, B. L. (2011). Where are the White girls? A qualitative analysis of how six African American girls made meaning of their sexuality, race and gender through the lens of rap. In D. Carlson & D. Roseboro (Eds.), *The sexuality curriculum: Youth culture, popular culture, and progressive sexuality education* (pp. 122–135). New York: Peter Lang Publishing.

SPALDING

*Chapter One*

# Repaying My Debt Through Context

"Besides God and family, you my life's jewel"
—The Roots featuring Common,
"Act Too (The Love of My Life)"

In my youth, I learned how to navigate the inner-city streets, the basketball court, and a dysfunctional family guided by the sounds that blasted from my radio. When OutKast said that I needed to "git up, get out, and git somthin," I started my first job on my sixteenth birthday; when Nas proclaimed that the world was mine, I went after it; after Jay-Z said to never live with regrets, I never looked back. I looked upon these MCs as an extended family of sorts and referred to all of them as my "uncles." Their gritty urban rhymes and 'hood stories of drugs, crime, violence, and womanizing— alongside tales of determination, strength, and overcoming obstacles—mimicked the conditions and raw emotions that were a common theme framing my neighborhood and many other communities across the United States in the early '80s and late '90s. In this way, Hip Hop served as my own personal tutor. I went to school for my formal education and listened to Hip Hop for my street education; to me, they are of equal importance. I was a youngster searching for answers, and Hip Hop explained to me why violence was taking over the streets on which I used to play and how drugs had dismantled my family and the families of my friends. More importantly, Hip Hop provided a lens for making sense of my environment and, ultimately, a means to deal with watching my community's soul decaying right before my eyes. Through this book, I hope to pay back a small portion of my debt to Hip Hop. I feel I owe it to Hip Hop to explain its significance and the way it shapes the lives of urban Black young girls who, like me, learned more from Hip Hop and Black popular culture than from twelve years of attending America's public schools.

This book is not about the use of Hip Hop in the classroom. It is about what happens when schools ignore Hip Hop, critical pedagogy, and culturally relevant teaching practices, and the consequences of failing to integrate Hip Hop and media literacy into urban classrooms. I often attend presentations and speeches on the state of Hip Hop at which many scholars, teachers, and community leaders speak to the promise of infusing rap music into the school curriculum or programs for at-risk teens, but rarely do they discuss how youth make meaning of rap, especially young Black girls. There is a definite need for studies that investigate the contextual surroundings, culture, and identity development of urban girls. Much of the academic dialogue on Hip Hop lacks honest conversations with young people that would provide empirical data regarding rap as an omnipresent "common culture" of youth—particularly young women of color—who have a muddled, impulsive, and discernible bond to the music and culture of rap (Dimitriadis, 2001; Kellner, 1998). As academics, we have to conduct research with the very youth who are the subjects of our theories and incorporate their voices into the discussion. The text of Hip Hop is alive, along with the constructions of race, class, gender, and sexuality that emerge as "spaces for resistance and negotiation" (Dimitriadis, 2001, p. 11).

This book aims to (1) trigger a dialogue that examines the complexities of Hip Hop music and culture and how these complexities impact Black girls; (2) examine my own research limitations stemming from my positionality as a queer, Northern-born researcher investigating Southern straight girls and its negative impact on my initial relationship with the girls; and (3) demonstrate the power of Hip Hop to transform urban education into a space that challenges students to examine their community and social positions via the music and culture of Hip Hop. The stage for this book is Atlanta, Georgia, the center of Southern-flavored Hip Hop music and culture. But Atlanta is more than just music; it stands as a city defined by Black and Brown folks who counter-culturally inform the American sociopolitical landscape and, through music, the world. Thus, the city of Atlanta is as much a part of this book as I am or as are the six young girls within who understand Hip Hop music and culture through Southern-tinted lenses.

## My Story

I came of age on the heels of Hip Hop. Born in 1979 in Rochester, New York, I am a true '80s baby. My family was like every other hardworking family in my neighborhood: predominantly Black, parents working forty hours–plus a week to pay the bills and keep food on the table, mothers cleaning the house every Saturday from top to bottom with Pine-Sol listening to Frankie Beverly and Maze, and constantly battling the temptations of drugs and alcohol that were biting away at their idea of the American Dream. While my story is unfortunately not unique, the cultural contributions of my generation are wholly our own. The phenomenon of Hip Hop emerged in the decade of Reaganomics—President Ronald Reagan's political attack on the poor and disadvantaged. By manipulating Americans with fear slogans like "War on Crime," "War on Drugs," "welfare queens," and "gang wars," Reagan's tactics helped cultivate the brash, gritty, often rebellious sound and culture of Hip Hop. Often called the Hip Hop generation (composed of individuals born just after the Civil Rights Movement), my generation grew out of bankrupt, economically deprived inner cities left virtually penniless when American jobs went overseas, tax cuts went to the wealthy, and millions of children of color were living in poverty (Rose, 1994; Zinn, 2005). The politics of the Reagan administration widened the wealth and achievement gaps, exacerbated the degradation of living standards for people of color, and intensified insufficient school funding, which ultimately eliminated many public school music programs. The wars on drugs and crime took place on almost every corner of my block and throughout inner-city streets across America. I learned to live between two rival gangs, saw many of my male friends resort to selling drugs, and watched as moms, dads, and my friends' brothers and sisters morphed into fiends walking the streets. In this way, the community context in which Hip Hop was conceived and matured is just as important as the music—it is the music.

At the core of this book lies the political, social, and local community context that I used to explain the events that shaped my life, which, not by coincidence, also shaped the lives of the six girls in my study. The inner-city spaces and politics that influenced Hip Hop music and culture impacted me as I came of age in the '80s and '90s and similarly affected the teenage girls within this book as they struggled to find their way in today's early twenty-first-century society. Today's youth are under attack by thugs in designer suits who use media outlets instead of street corners to destroy the developing minds of teenagers, particularly the minds of Black youth. As a kid, I can remember being angry and longing for answers. I wondered why my neighborhood and household had changed. I wanted to know the reasons behind the new monthly visits of "Officer Friendly" and his message to "Just Say No" to drugs (also known to '80s babies as D.A.R.E.—Drug Abuse Resistance Education). Yearning to know where all the mothers and fathers went, including my own, I had no one to turn to but my "uncles." Schools seemed to ignore the urban terrain around my friends and me and failed to acknowledge the life circumstances that affected us as students.

Growing up with a basketball in one hand and a radio in the other, I landed myself an athletic scholarship, one of the few options for youth growing up in urban areas. I left Rochester armed with street knowledge and just enough formal education to attempt college. During my early college years, I had no real aspirations other than playing basketball and listening to Hip Hop, but my hoop dreams eventually deflated, and I was left only with the music and culture of my youth—truly the only culture that felt natural. As my focus began to turn from basketball to academics, I started to question why all of my educators largely ignored something that was so important to me and had taught me so much. Realizing this deficiency, I began to envision elementary classrooms where Hip Hop music and culture were part of school curriculum. After earning a Master's degree in Elementary Education and taking my first teaching job, I started listening to Hip Hop as a critical consumer, which was, for me, a newly discovered viewpoint. I realized that I had never questioned the music that I adored or even, for that matter, my own culture. I continually dismissed the sexist, violent, and homophobic nature of Hip Hop because I was unaware of how the music impacted me. At the time, I was not ready to question why my "'hood story" of growing up surrounded by violence, drugs, and a dysfunctional family filled me with such a sense of pride and bonded me to a genre of music that provided an inside look into a world that I both loved and hated. In short, I did not want to question why I felt that my hardships as a youth authenticated my Blackness.

My romanticized views of the music and culture left me trapped between my youth and adulthood: I was not only a first-year teacher with professional responsibilities but also a young adult, which are two worlds that can be confusing and difficult to navigate just by themselves. While I was starting to understand how Hip Hop impacted my life, my students' interactions with the music differed from my own, or so I thought. As I moved from student to teacher, I became critical of Hip Hop culture and instituted my own elitist parameters around the music whereby I made the narrow-minded distinction between rap (low culture) and Hip Hop (high culture). I saw rap as the music of my students and Hip Hop as my music. I fell into the trap of viewing my students through a deficit cultural lens. I forgot about context and blamed rap music for their shortcomings. Looking back, I was no better than rap critics Stanley Crouch (2006) or John McWhorter (2003), who ignore the urban milieu in which Black urban teens consume rap. Crouch and McWhorter's thinking blames youth of color for their plight and dismisses the music as being created by circumstances beyond an inner-city kid's control. As a teacher who was steadily reaching middle-class status and each day waking up more removed from my past than before, I overlooked issues of poverty, police brutality, corporate greed, and racially biased mandatory sentencing laws that Black and Brown youth encounter. I simplified the struggles of my students by attributing their pitfalls to apathetic parents and a young society driven by the excessive "bling-bling" culture of rap—two easy scapegoats for novice teachers unwilling to acknowledge teacher failure after years of formal training.

After months of soul searching and failing to meet the cultural needs of my students, I came to recognize the hypocrisy in my role reversal as I saw my students' music as something disconnected from Hip Hop culture. Since their music did not sound like Digable Planets, Talib Kweli, De La Soul, or Poor Righteous Teachers, I dissed and dismissed it. In doing so, I created a hierarchy between my rap music and that of my students. Since many of them, if not all, were unaware of the original roots of Hip Hop and the elements that created Hip Hop music and culture (Emceeing/rapping/Mcing, Deejaying, Break dancing or Bboying/Bgirling, Graffiti art/tagging, and Knowledge of self), I positioned the music of my students as less than "real" Hip Hop because their music did not embody the elements of Hip Hop in its entirety. They only embraced rap, which is one of the fundamental creative pillars of Hip Hop culture but not the entirety of the culture itself. My students' understanding of Hip Hop was fragmented, much like their knowledge of what it means to be of African American or of African descent. I decided to meet my students in the middle of the commercialization of Hip Hop that created this fragmentation. When I stopped calling their music garbage, I began to listen and find commonalities between the messages of their music and mine. To me, the music shared the same anger, frustration, fears, and romanticized yet critical observations of Black and Brown communities filled with drugs, guns, and violence. Thus, although at first it seemed unfamiliar, when I explored my students' music with a more incisive ear I discovered that it echoed the systemic sociopolitical problems that I faced as a child—the same problems that were plaguing my students. I came to realize that the only difference between me and my students was that I had made it out of my community that had been overtaken by drugs, violence, and low-performing schools, which are all byproducts of America's failure to provide jobs, adequate schools, and safe streets to working class and poor communities. This failure is the result of failed or inadequate social and educational policies that ignore years of oppression and fall short in attempts to genuinely end poverty and poor schooling.

Although I had some successes in the classroom, it was not enough to deem myself a potential master teacher. I was again left with questions regarding the power and potential of Hip Hop. However, this time I discovered new family members—"uncles" and "aunts"—beyond the world of Hip Hop who spoke a new language that provided an analytical critique of the issues my students and I experienced as inner-city kids.

While completing my doctoral work in Social Foundations of Education, I discovered a group of scholars who had already learned to critique their own experiences with Black popular culture: Tricia Rose, Stuart Hall, bell hooks, Henry Giroux, Joe L. Kincheloe, Patricia Hill Collins, Murray Forman, Audre Lorde, James Baldwin, Michael Eric Dyson, Gwendolyn D. Pough, Mark Anthony Neal, Aisha Durham, Kristal Brent Zook, Robin D. G. Kelley, Nelson George, Elaine Richardson, Sister Souljah, David Stovall, Shirley Steinberg, Greg Dimitriadis, Marc Lamont Hill, Joan Morgan, Derrick Alridge, and Cornel West. These scholars inspired me to question my sentimental perceptions of Hip Hop and see it as an artistic, complex, and commodified form of Black popular culture that impacts our youth and informs their identities. I began utilizing Hall's (1983) definition of Black popular culture as my theoretical foundation, which he stated as being:

> the space of homogenizations where stereotyping and the formulaic mercilessly process the material and experiences it draws into its web, where control over narratives and representations passes into hands of established cultural bureaucracies, sometimes without a murmur. It is rooted in popular experience and available for expropriation at one and the same time. (p. 26)

Hall's perspective helped me to understand more fully how and why I initially came to assume that the rap music my students listened to was inferior and seemed to bear little to no resemblance to the Hip Hop music and culture of my youth. I discovered that these were misguided assumptions as I came to understand the music and culture through a historical and sociopolitical perspective. This new perspective was also guided by the scholarship of Collins (2004), who argues that Black popular culture is an element of mass media, which through visual and audio representations of Black sexuality reproduces messages of social inequality, racism, sexism, classism, and capitalism. These scholars helped me develop a framework that stopped blaming students and parents for what I believed to be shortcomings. I turned my focus to the hegemonic representations of Black life that Black youth consume and interpret, especially young Black girls. Through Black popular culture and mass media, "slavery and its legacy of racial rules" (Richardson, 2007, p. 790) are repackaged to produce stereotypical and hegemonic representations of women of color. Black girls, as consumers of Black popular culture, and in particular Hip Hop music and culture, are reading the text and negotiating, resisting, succumbing, and finding spaces for contradictions of the stereotypical images of Black life.

My motivation for writing this book spans my life experiences, from a teenager enthralled with the street-prophet MCs of my youth to a passionate adult researcher and educator. Through my work with urban youth, particularly young girls of color, I know that before I can successfully integrate Hip Hop into the classroom, I need to understand how music and culture influence the youth's perceptions of race, gender, and sexuality as framed by societal norms. Rap is not created in an urban vacuum, untouched by society and its social constructs. Rap's materialistic, sexist, racist, and homophobic qualities, as well as its insatiable greed, stem from branches rooted within our society. It is an extension of American culture and is influenced by America's urban streets, corporate boardrooms, and youth of all colors.

Just as Hip Hop takes its cues from society so too do its young consumers. The underlying context of this book is a sociopolitical examination of how six young Black girls from Atlanta, Georgia, understood Hip Hop. These girls' stories, which I illuminate within the pages of this book, like mine, are not uncommon. Unfortunately, too many of our Black and Brown girls live in poverty-stricken neighborhoods, under siege by their own communities and by Black popular culture. However, unique to girls of color today are the ways in which they make meaning of their circumstances, consume Black popular culture, and conceptualize inequality, merit, sexuality, race, privilege, and body image through social constructs echoed within rap and their local community and city of Atlanta. This work investigates the "Pimps Up, Ho's Down" (Sharpley-Whiting, 2007) mantra of rap music through these six girls' lives. It is important as educators, parents, and pedagogues that we know how young women construe the formulaic space of rap that is controlled by so many hands and influenced by America's pejorative societal norms. With these issues in mind, the ethnographic study presented within this book sought to understand how six African American female teens, ages thirteen to seventeen, conceptualized rap music through the lens of rap videos, lyrics, and societal beliefs that stem from the majority. Their interactions with Hip Hop are important not only for the study of Black girlhood but also for determining how young women growing up in our inner cities interpret social constructs of race, gender, sexuality, merit, body image, politics, and success. The six young women within these pages illustrate the complexities and contradictions of Hip Hop and society, and the real-life implications of the music, from the viewpoint of Hip Hop's "li'l sistas." However, there is a seventh woman within the book: me. I am also one of Hip Hop's li'l sistas, a little older, I hope a little wiser, but still wrestling with the intricacies and ambiguities of Hip Hop music, culture, and social constructs that have for better or for worse informed my thinking throughout my life. This book documents my love for Hip Hop in conjunction with my passion for researching Black girlhood, but what I hope to share in addition to the voices of urban Black girls are my pitfalls as a researcher and human that initially shaped my relationship with the girls.

## ATL*iens*

To many, Atlanta is known as "The ATL," which stems from Atlanta's airport code and its global popularity. While Atlanta is home to the busiest airport in the United States, ATL also garners its popularity as the name younger Atlantans use to describe home, due in large part to the rap community. In 1996 OutKast, Atlanta's number-one-selling rap group, released their second studio album entitled *ATLiens*. The album's portmanteau title highlighted Atlanta's uniqueness as a city and its distinctive musical sound, which catapulted Atlanta, its Southern roots, and Black folks who call Atlanta home into the global phenomenon of Hip Hop. The six girls who participated in the research project are ATLiens: They speak with a Southern drawl, are proud of their Atlanta roots, and are shaped by the city's politics, race relations, public schools, economics, culture, and music.

## The Girls

I met all the youth who participated in this study while working at a local community center called Hope Community Center (HCC) in 2005. The name of the center and the names of the girls have been changed to protect their identity. I worked with the girls for two years at HCC as a staff member and basketball coach before I started researching the six girls and three boys for my dissertation in 2007. I did not include the boys who participated in the study because they did not take part in the discussions regarding the issues addressed within the book.

*Fearless*, *blunt*, and *confident*—if pressed to describe the Johnson girls in three words, with one word representing each sister, these are the words I would choose. The Johnson girls consist of seventeen-year-old twins Nicole and Lara and fifteen-year-old Lisa. Initially, my interaction with the Johnson girls was an intense fight for mutual respect. As a staff member at HCC, my job was to ensure that they completed their homework, an often daunting task, because Nicole and Lara used every excuse in the book to avoid it. Lisa, on the other hand, was an above-average student who excelled at school and was enrolled in a number of Advanced Placement classes. Aside from those daily disputes, one of the biggest disagreements between the girls and me centered around language. They constantly used matronly endearments like "honey" and "baby" when referring to youth and adults alike. The more I insisted that the girls call me by my name, Tina or Coach T, the more it became apparent that "Honey" was my new name.

Each of the girls was extremely confident, quick witted, and unafraid of speaking her mind. Lisa was the overachiever of the family and had a high grade point average. She was placed in classes such as Advanced Placement Biology and Spanish III. She was playful but respectful. She was the fighter in the family and spoke up for her sisters, which I found ironic because she was the youngest. Lisa liked school and wanted more than anything to go to college. At the time of the study, she spoke to me about leaving home to attend college and the financial costs it would entail. Lisa was the calm, levelheaded one who was not afraid of anyone and was determined to make a better life for herself.

Nicole was the younger of the twins. She was by far the most outspoken of the three. Conversely, she could be caring and motherly, which contributed to her becoming a good leader. Academically, Nicole's performance directly contrasted to Lisa's. Nicole struggled to pass her classes. She also had plans for the future—she considered becoming a chef or a teacher, and she wanted to go to college. Lara was the older twin. She loved to engage anyone in a conversation and could talk herself out of almost any situation at HCC. Although she struggled in school, she too wanted a college education.

Star, age fourteen, stood almost 5'9" and was one of the tallest teens at the center. She loved to entertain. Star had so much personality; she made sure she spoke to everyone who walked into the center. She was an average student—her grades were fair, and she always avoided trouble. Star spent much of her time at the center with her friend Maxine. Star and Maxine were like most fourteen-year-old girls who love talking on the phone, buying clothes, learning the latest dances, and listening to music. Maxine, also fourteen, was a ball of energy and never stopped talking or moving. Maxine was athletic and one of the few girls who enjoyed playing sports. Dee, age sixteen, was the critical thinker of the group. Dee was always deep in thought. Dee was an above-average student, but her true love was playing the clarinet in her school's band.

## Researching Cultural Consumption

The core research questions that grounded this study were concerned with how young Black girls at HCC constructed identities through the rap music present in their everyday lives. The guiding research questions were the following:

1. How do girls understand the images presented in rap music and rap videos?

2. How do rap's messages contribute to the girls' construction of racial and gender identities?

3. How does rap music shape the girls' lived experiences?

In order to investigate these research questions, I applied ethnographic methods to understanding the girls' cultural consumption of rap. I conducted formal group and individual interviews, along with observations and countless impromptu interviews, that spanned sixteen months of data collection. My data served as my guide into the lives of Lisa, Lara, Nicole, Maxine, Star, and Dee. By the end of the study, I had spent a year and a half as a researcher in addition to my two years as a staff member at the community center. I visited the site two to three times a week, every week, for roughly three hours per visit, not including the weekend programs that I attended.

## Methodology

Interviews were the primary source of data and, therefore, the heart of the study. The interviews consisted of semi-structured and unstructured open-ended questions. I constructed many of the interview questions on an ongoing basis because they pertained to each student's experiences with rap music. I also conducted group interviews, which I found to be quite helpful, as the participants spoke candidly with their peers about issues and experiences. Merriam (1998) maintains that a good respondent is "one who understands the culture but is also able to reflect on it and articulate for the researcher what is going on" (p. 85). As regards to formal interviews, I conducted eight individual interviews and four group interviews with Lisa; nine individual interviews and four group interviews with Dee; six individual interviews and three group interviews with Maxine; five individual interviews and three group interviews with Star; five individual interviews and two group interviews with Lara; and eight individual interviews and three group interviews with Nicole. After conducting interviews, transcribing the data, editing my transcripts, and reading over my data, I used the "open coding" method to analyze my data. The process of "open coding" is that of organizing data into "chunks" that represent categories, oftentimes based on the actual language of the participant (Creswell, 2003). While coding my data, I wrote countless memos to reflect on the substantive issues and summarize my observer comments. These memos served as the analysis foundation as I began to ask myself analytic questions in order to create themes, grounded first in my codes and then in the literature. The analytic questions focused on the process and the meaning of the words and actions of my participants. The questions helped me examine my data beyond a surface-level analysis. While coding data and writing memos, I asked myself why the youth of HCC had a one-dimensional notion of Blackness. How did the center's location and tutor population foster meaning making for the students? How did the city of Atlanta influence the girls' perceptions? And why did the participants believe that a particular body type and expression of sexuality was being a "real" Black woman? These questions helped me take my data from categorized codes and "chunks" to representational themes, which I could ground in literature that provided an explanation to my data. My codes are found on the figure on page 12. These codes, along with the analytic questions, helped me create code families to examine my data and place them within theoretical perspectives.

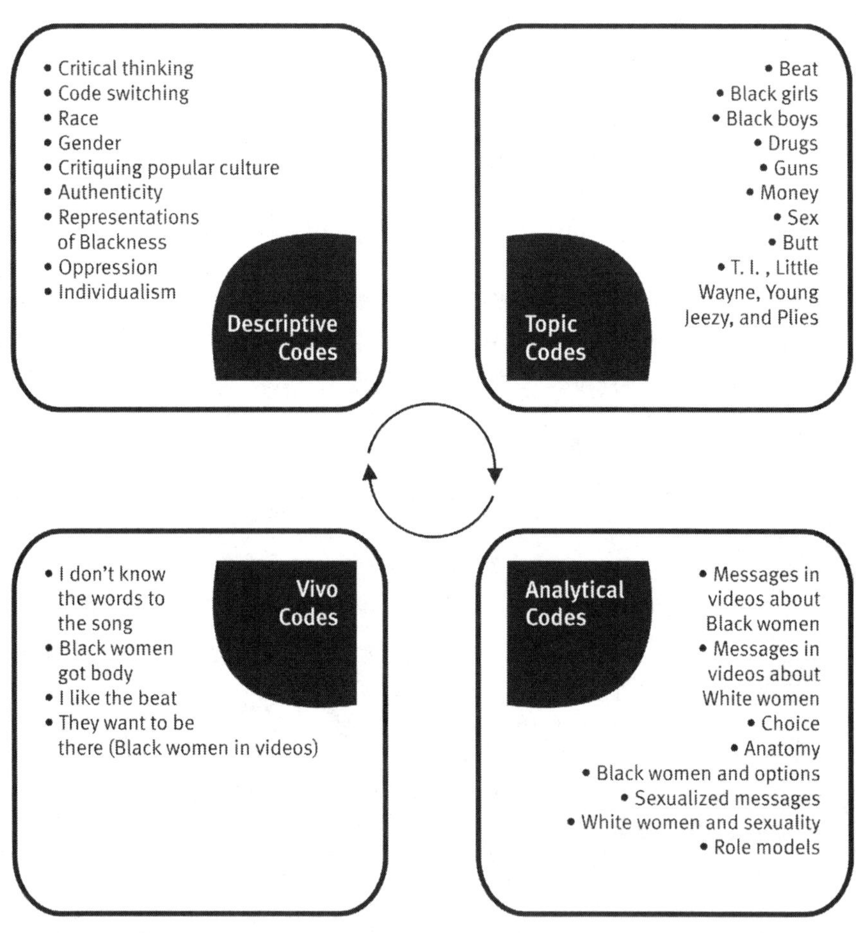
• Critical thinking
• Code switching
• Race
• Gender
• Critiquing popular culture
• Authenticity
• Representations of Blackness
• Oppression
• Individualism
Descriptive Codes
• Beat
• Black girls
• Black boys
• Drugs
• Guns
• Money
• Sex
• Butt
• T. I. , Little Wayne, Young Jeezy, and Plies
Topic Codes
• I don't know the words to the song
• Black women got body
• I like the beat
• They want to be there (Black women in videos)
Vivo Codes
Analytical Codes
• Messages in videos about Black women
• Messages in videos about White women
• Choice
• Anatomy
• Black women and options
• Sexualized messages
• White women and sexuality
• Role models

## Researching in My Own Backyard

When I originally asked the girls to be a part of the study, their initial responses were, "Why us?" and "You want to interview us?" Of course, my reply was, "Why not?" After that encounter, I realized that many of the girls had never been asked what they thought about Hip Hop or, typical of societal engagement with girls (and girls of color especially), had never been asked what they thought about anything of substance, for that matter. I had known the girls for almost two years as their basketball coach and as a staff member of HCC before I started the research project. Most of the girls did not want to play basketball, but it was part of the summer camp program when I started working at HCC in the summer of 2005. During these two years, I realized that their voices were absent from scholarly and community discussions on Hip Hop music and culture, especially in Atlanta. Thus, I thought it was necessary, even though it might mean academic suicide, to research in my own backyard.

When I started to seriously consider conducting my dissertation research at the center, I had questions regarding objectivity (at this time in my life I thought being objective was possible), my ethical responsibility to the center and the youth, and, more generally, positions of power. In an effort to resolve these issues, I drew from research approaches that advocated cultural sensitivity.

1. Recognize ethnicity and position culture at the center of the research process (Denzin & Lincoln, 1994; Dillard, 2000; Tillman, 2002).
2. Place collective knowledge of African Americans at the center of the inquiry (Tillman, 2002).
3. Seek opportunities for collaboration, insider perspectives, reciprocity, and voice (Tillman, 2002).
4. Remember the importance of connectedness between the researcher and the research community (Dillard, 2000).
5. Focus on uncovering and discovering the multiple realities and experiences of African Americans (Dillard, 2000; Tillman, 2002).

These perspectives were central to how I viewed my research location and the youngsters in the study. I also knew that my shifting of roles would complicate my lenses as a researcher, but it would also allow me to "work the hyphen," which "suggests that researchers probe who we are in relation with the context we study and with our informants, understanding that we are all multiple in those relations . . . to see how these 'relations between' get us 'better' data" (Fine, 1994, p. 72). My multiple roles—staff member, volunteer, tutor, and researcher—and identities—Black, queer, and female—shaped my research as I entered HCC as an "embodied knowledge-producing agent" (Dimitriadis, 2001, p. 578). However, I am now fully aware that three constructs limited my work: my internalized homophobia; my opinions of Southerners, which were instilled in me as a child growing up in upstate New York and followed me into early adulthood; and my perception of the influence of the Southern Black church on Atlanta's youth culture, which will all be discussed in Chapter Four.

The six girls within this book are all complex and intelligent, with fluid identities that are partially shaped by the city of Atlanta. The city these young ladies call home is built on racism, sexism, classism, conspicuous consumption, the sex industry, low-performing public schools, poverty, and crime, as well as the Civil Rights Movement, social conservatism, Christianity, gospel, soul, rhythm and blues, pop, neo soul, snap, crunk, and Southern Hip Hop. In this sense, Atlanta also has unexplainable and indestructible strength, beauty, pride, and communal love that are as unique as the city is. Thus, this book attempts to take the aforementioned factors into account to illustrate the ways in which six Black young females made meaning of Hip Hop music and culture—dirty South style. Chapter Two sets the stage for my work as a cultural theorist who examines Hip Hop from the contrived space of its commercialization and my multiple identities as researcher, educator, and feminist. Chapter Three chronicles Atlanta's rise to the global popular culture spotlight and what that transformation means for the city's Black female youth. Chapter Four narrates my fears and struggles in researching Black girls as a queer researcher while trying to address my internalized homophobia and stereotypes of Southerners and the Southern Black church. Chapters Five and Six, through qualitative data, illustrate how Lara, Dee, Nicole, Star, Maxine, and Lisa conceptualized Hip Hop music and culture within the space of Atlanta to inform their notions of self, body image, gender, race, and politics. Specifically, Chapter Five highlights how historical-political ideologies and rhetoric, beyond the party lines of Democrat and Republican, shape America's ideas of success in order to inform the youth about race and merit as they make judgments about Black women who participate in rap videos. Chapter Six outlines the girls' understanding of the Black female body and how their male counterparts found them desirable or not in comparison to women who appeared in rap videos. Chapter Seven highlights how the virulent beat of rap became hegemonic for the girls; they adored rap music for the beat but ignored its problematic messages because of the beat and the pressure to fit in with their peers. Finally, Chapter Eight discusses how the girls resisted some of Hip Hop's more pugnacious messages, chronicles Hip Hop's transformation from my generation to the generation of the girls in the study, and argues that schools must be the space that cultivates media-literate girls.

A

*Chapter Two*

# Hip Hop, Context, and Black Girlhood

The context in which youth consume rap is often dismissed, along with systemic conditions of racism and sexism, systematic criminalization, culturally biased high-stakes testing, and ideologies of merit and privilege (Fine & Ruglis, 2009). Some scholars, like Crouch (2006), Ford (2002), and McWhorter (2003), write passionately from the posture that Hip Hop is a threat to Black youth. These authors argue that rap music reinforces negative stereotypes, which hinder the social, economic, and educational progress of Black youth in America. In "What's Holding Blacks Back?," McWhorter (2003) related the story of an afternoon lunch at a Kentucky Fried Chicken in Harlem. He watched a group of Black teenage boys "check out of mainstream society" (p. 1). He further described the boys' behavior as "bellicose" and suggested that they demonstrated a "bone-deep dislike of authority" (p. 1). McWhorter then drew a direct correlation between the boys' behavior and Hip Hop culture and rap music, stating that:

> many writers and thinkers see a kind of informed political engagement, even revolutionary potential, in rap and hip hop. They couldn't be more wrong. By reinforcing the stereotypes that long hindered blacks, and by teaching young blacks that a thuggish adversarial stance is the properly "authentic" response to a presumptively racist society, rap retards black success. (2003, p. 2)

McWhorter, like many of rap's critics, failed to tackle rap from a larger perspective. I question whether rap holds the sole blame for "retard[ing]" Blacks when corporate America, the failing structure of public education, the for-profit prison industry, and the contrived media have urban youth and rap in a tight chokehold. Without context, it is easy to label Black and Brown youth as "bellicose" and justify the injustices against them. For example, during the 1980s and 1990s state spending for corrections increased six times faster than spending for higher education. Today, one in fifteen Black men and one in thirty-six Latino men are behind bars (Dyson, 2010). So long as scholars and cultural critics fail to critically interrogate urban youth and rap music, jointly, within the discourses of capitalism, hegemony, poverty, media and cultural studies, politics, and domination, urban youth of color will remain society's scapegoat (Alexander, 2010; Giroux, 2003; Hill, 2009; Omi & Winant, 1994). Too often, sophisticated systems of oppression are negated when researching the plight of Black and Brown youth. A working example is the hegemony where domination is maintained through "contemporary democratic societies not through the use of force, but through winning the consent of the people" (Kincheloe, 2002, p. 129). Through hegemony, Hip Hop is created in a contrived space where the commodification of Blackness perpetuates the status quo and existing social structures of inequality. Corporate boardrooms create much of rap's music and culture, and they then mask and disseminate it to youth as street culture or "real" Hip Hop. For example, rap moguls like Sean "Diddy" Combs, Jermaine Dupri, and Percy "Master P" Miller share a large majority of their profits with major record labels (Love, 2010). Sociologist Dipannita Basu (2005) contends that "major corporate conglomerates control the music industry. . . . Black rap moguls exist, but the industry is white controlled" (p. 258). To be blunt, if rappers want to be financially successful they will structure their performances, image, lyrics, and videos to parallel the White imagination. According to West (2001), the entertainment industry mainstreamed rap by bombarding the music "with the racist stereotypes of black men as hypercriminal and hypersexual and black women as willing objects of their conquest" (p. 181). This assertion is evident as one scans popular rap songs, which glorify crime, violence, homophobia, and promiscuity. Dyson (1996) argues that it is "easier to get an album made if you're 'pimpin' hoes, 'cockin' glocks,' or generally 'bitch-baiting'" than if you're "promoting Black unity or the overthrow of white racism" (p. 114). Lupe Fiasco's brilliant song, "Dumb It Down," supports Dyson's claim.

*You've been shedding too much light Lu (Dumb it down)*
*You make 'em wanna do right Lu (Dumb it down)*
*They're getting self-esteem Lu (Dumb it down)*
*These girls are trying to be queens Lu (Dumb it down)*
*They're trying to graduate from school Lu (Dumb it down)*
*They're starting to think that smart is cool Lu (Dumb it down)*
*They're trying to get up out the hood Lu (Dumb it down)*
*I'll tell you what you should do (Dumb it down)*

Through these lyrics, Lupe Fiasco exposes how a large majority of record companies only promote rap artists who are willing to bolster negative stereotypes of people of color that maintain oppressive social positions. This maintenance of domination is even more evident upon examination of the depictions of females of color within Hip Hop. The hypersexual representations of women, coupled with debasing racial and gender social constructs, translate into how a number of young Black women see themselves, other women of color, and non-Black women.

### Venus Versus Mars

> The misogynist lyrics of gangsta rap are hateful indeed, but they do not represent a new trend in Black popular culture, nor do they differ fundamentally from woman-hating discourses that are common among White men. The danger of this insight is that it might be read as an apology for Black misogyny.
>
> —Leola Johnson (1996, p. 10)

In the backdrop of Hip Hop stand young women of color who are cast as video vixens, strippers, hos, baby mommas, groupies, bitches, and models—each a mere accessory to male rappers. Through recent rap music and Black popular culture, women of color are more visible now than ever before, even though they have always been a fundamental part of Hip Hop music and culture. However, rap's trend of sexism and misogyny—systemic within capitalism and patriarchy, which are part of America's ethos (Adams & Fuller, 2006; hooks, 1994)—degrades the dynamic, fundamental roles women of color have within Hip Hop. hooks (1994) explains the convoluted relationship between race, gender, and patriarchy here:

> The sexist, misogynist, patriarchal ways of thinking and behaving that are glorified in gangsta rap are a reflection of the prevailing values in our society, values created and sustained by white supremacist capitalist patriarchy. As the crudest and most brutal expression of sexism, misogynistic attitudes tend to be portrayed by the dominant culture as an expression of male deviance. In reality they are part of a sexist continuum, necessary for the maintenance of patriarchal social order. (p. 2)

As a consequence of its mainstream success, rap's lyrical and visual assault on women of color goes beyond gangsta or commercial rap. The sexualized representations of Black women within Hip Hop are a permanent fixture due to the institutionalized sexism proliferated by the dominant culture. Tackling the nuances of Hip Hop in her book, *The Hip Hop Wars*, Tricia Rose (2008) states, "We live and breathe in a world that normalizes sexism. . . . Sexism sells, mostly because we refuse to fight sexism with any seriousness" (p. 172). In that same vein, the work of Mako Fitts (2008) adds empirical evidence to the claims of hooks and Rose. Fitts (2008) examined the "cultural industry laborers" of rap by interviewing industry insiders (music video directors, casting directors, and video girls). Fitts found that both males and females subjected women to "harsh physical scrutiny" and viewed them as "commodities" (p. 219). One insider told Fitts that in casting for rap videos, "[i]t's all about the hot girls." The selection of these so-called hot girls reinforces gendered and racialized stereotypes. By simply scanning many popular rap videos, the sexual landscape becomes clear in the monolithic imaging of Black and Brown women dressed in little to nothing, dancing as sexual objects without emotions or words.

Within the climate of rap, women of color—and their bodies—are a vital part of a racialized fantasy world. This phenomenon is best illustrated by their appearance in "booty videos" that highlight Black women's posteriors (Fitts, 2008). Arnett (2002) describes these videos as "one or more men performing while beautiful, scantily clad young women dance and writhe lasciviously... The women are mostly just props, not characters, not even people really" (p. 256). Fitts contends that rap's muse is the provocative playground of strip clubs, where women are on display for patrons' viewing pleasure. In rap culture, this explicit sexual imagery sells more than just sex and male fantasies; it maintains women of color as racial commodities who are sexually deviant and erotic. The race-specific sophisticated marketing of rap music by corporate America transmits more than just 'hood stories of violence, gangs, crime, and womanizing. It draws from a legacy of patriarchy, corporate greed, and the White exoticization of the Black female body in order to portray women of color and Black sexuality as an "illicit erotic economy" (Miller-Young, 2008, p. 261). Kelley (1998) suggests that for urban youth, "capitalism has become both their greatest friend and greatest foe" (p. 77). For women of color, capitalism and Hip Hop serve simultaneously as a loving father, supportive husband, courageous brother, kind son, and abusive, manipulative pimp.

As a member of the Hip Hop generation, a Black woman, and a lesbian, I grapple with my affection for rap due to its competing themes—of pleasure, love, homophobia, sexism, and misogyny. However, like Pough (2002), "[m]y development as a Black women and a Black feminist is deeply tied to my love of hip hop" (p. 86). Although my "uncles" were instrumental in shaping my knowledge and understanding regarding what it means to grow up urban, angry, disenfranchised, and yet resilient, it was female MCs who taught me how to love my community and find my voice within the male bravado of rap and society at large. Lauryn Hill helped me develop my Black female consciousness. Her music taught me how to feel, give of myself, and critique my "uncles." While I enjoyed female MCs like Salt-N-Pepa, Queen Latifah, and MC Lyte, I never fully identified with their messages about dating and romance when discussing men—though admittedly I knew every word to "Whatta Man" by Salt-N-Pepa. The music of those female MCs taught me how to demand respect, talk back to sexism, and think like a Black feminist before I even knew to call myself one. Now I listen to rap as a Hip Hop feminist who understands that capitalism and patriarchy have had profound impact on the music and that sex and gender are "powerful organizing social constructs" (Jeffries, 2007, p. 212) that have placed women in subordinate positions to their male counterparts. My multiple identities as researcher, educator, feminist, and Hip Hop Head have inspired my investigation of young Black girls' understanding of rap. Peoples (2008) argues that "hip-hop feminists contend that hip-hop is also a site where young black women begin or further develop their own gender critique and feminist identity, which they can then turn toward the misogyny of rap music" (p. 21). I believe this lofty goal is obtainable, but educators, parents, and community organizations must equip young girls of color with the proper tools necessary to challenge, as women, the misogyny prevalent in this genre of music, which is such an integral aspect of their youth. One tool that can help young girls examine rap is the lens of Hip Hop feminism, which can be a contentious space for many women of color but is a space that is crucial in critiquing rap and crafting Black female identity. As important as Hip Hop feminism is to the empowerment of today's Black urban teens, the intersection and/or collusion of feminism and Hip Hop can provoke contention between and among feminist thinkers of color.

## Black Feminism, Lesbianism, and Hip Hop Feminism

> Young women are struggling with the feminist label, not only, as some prominent Second Wavers have asserted, because we lack a knowledge of women's history and have been alienated by the media's generally horrific characterization of feminists...Young women coming of age today wrestle with the term because we have a very different vantage point on the world than that of our foremothers.
>
> —Rebecca Walker (1995, pp. xxxii–xxxiii)

Over time, the word *feminism* has become a convoluted term that invokes contentious emotions and thoughts from individuals of all racial and ethnic backgrounds. I often hear women refer to feminism as the "F" word, as if to imply the word is comparable to swearing. Nonetheless, women of color who define themselves as feminist have found a comfortable space for the term, as Black feminist or womanist. These two terms, *Black feminist* and *womanist*, are used interchangeably because both terms draw on feminist theory as a mode of analysis but detach from feminist thought because of its hegemonic and racist past. Womanism became mainstream in 1983 when Alice Walker introduced the term in her definitive book *In Search of Our Mothers' Gardens: Womanist Prose.* Walker defined *womanism* as a perspective for social change that women of color could employ to critique their everyday experiences to fight injustice. Black feminism draws on the intersection of race, gender, class, sexuality, and national or transnational identity to think critically and challenge the historical and cultural oppression women of color face as they continue to endure racism, colonialism, and White supremacy. Black feminists are also concerned with the family and community structure in which youth of color learn and grow. Naturally, Black feminist concern and theory include the racialized space of Black popular culture, which is why Black feminism provides a foundational lens for my work.

The music and culture of my generation have equally influenced my lens as a Black feminist. My positionality and love for Hip Hop, alongside my sociopolitical views and criticisms of Hip Hop music and culture, situate me as a "daughter of feminist privilege" (Morgan, 1999, p. 59). Through Black feminism I can critique the patriarchal power within Hip Hop while finding pleasure in the music as a Hip Hop feminist. Hip Hop feminism allows a space within third-wave feminism for women and men who love Hip Hop to negotiate feminist thought, as they "refuse to be bound by a feminist ideal not of their own making" (Walker, 1995, p. xxxiv). shani jamila (2002) argues that "as women of the hip-hop generation we need a feminist consciousness that allows us to examine how representations and images can be simultaneously empowering and problematic" (p. 392). My lesbian identification allows me to add to Walker's critique of feminism, because this identification brings yet another set of reference points to feminism. Queer Black feminist Andreana Clay (2007) suggests that "[q]ueer women of color construct new meanings of text and become active consumers who change the context of sexuality and masculinity" (p. 158).

Lesbian researchers with a Hip Hop feminist posture blur the landscape of Hip Hop music and culture, sexuality, and masculinity. Thus, I examine how my sexuality and masculine embodiment or performance limited my research and placed an invisible wall between me and the girls in the study—a wall that I created and my participants knocked down. Hip Hop feminism's foundation rests within third-wave Black feminist thought, which challenges the social, political, and economic marginalization of women, especially those of color (Peoples, 2008). Pulling from the aforementioned strategies, Hip Hop feminism critiques more complex and contemporary issues facing women of color today, such as the hypermasculine, heteronormative, and xenophobic space of Hip Hop. Simply defined, Hip Hop feminism seeks to examine rap music and culture through a Black feminist lens that questions the misogyny and sexism within the art form but recognizes the sexual agency of women who utilize the culture to express themselves and their sexual desires. The unlikely marriage of Black feminism and Hip Hop allows contemporary Black women ambiguity and multiple positionalities (Peoples, 2008). Hip Hop feminism provides women and men with "the right to self-define feminist identities and praxis, yet the right to self-define, without a larger systemic strategy, can become an isolated and individual solution" (Peoples, 2008, p. 41). Hip Hop feminism embodies the complexities of love and pleasure and the critique of rap. For example, many of my friends—gay or straight—and I oppose vehemently the labeling of women as hos and bitches in rap songs, but we still dance to and purchase rap music with explicit lyrical content. I have even witnessed lesbians engage in relationships that mirror the same sexist and misogynic tone of male rappers. Clay (2007) suggests that "[t]he same objectification and violence toward women can happen regardless of the gender of the protagonist. And, queer communities are similar to the hip-hop community in that they reflect popular culture and discourse" (p. 160). That is why Jeffries (2007) argues that "hip-hop diehards with anti-sexist politics live in constant torment" (p. 208).

Needless to say, multiple positionalities within Hip Hop feminism exist in this book. There is no perfect formula to loving and critiquing Hip Hop; however, there is a dire need to understand how the most fragile, silent, and loving young women make meaning of an inner-city culture influenced heavily by mainstream society. This is why Hip Hop feminism, critical pedagogy, Hip Hop pedagogy, culturally relevant pedagogy, and media literacy are important components of any conversation regarding youth and popular culture, particularly Black popular culture, because it is the place where identities are constructed for people of color. When I enter schools or community centers to speak with youth about the media, I typically start off by asking students one particular question placed within a scenario (however, I did not ask the girls at the community center any questions like this one before my research project). I ask students to close their eyes and imagine an island far away, where no one has ever seen television or used the Internet or radio. While I do not disclose the race or skin color of the people on the island, because I believe it is irrelevant, I do however tell the students that the island residents have never seen a person of color before. Then, one day someone drops a big-screen television down on the island that is powered by solar energy, but it only has one channel—B.E.T. Then I ask the students, "What do you think the people on the island would think about the people on the T.V. channel?" The answers students give, regardless of their age, are comparable to what Crouch, McWhorter, Bill O'Reilly, and Rush Limbaugh would say, because they, too, make judgments about youth of color without understanding why those images are chosen to represent people of color. Some answers that I often get from students are, "They would think Black people are dumb"; They think Black people can only rap"; and "Black women don't wear any clothes." These answers to my loaded question tell me that students are critiquing rap music as informal cultural theorists. However, these conversations embedded within issues of race, class, gender, womanhood, exploitation, and sexuality are ignored or never nurtured in schools; no attempt is made to help students fully understand the music they consume. Critical pedagogy, Hip Hop pedagogy, culturally relevant pedagogy, Hip Hop feminism, and media literacy, which I explore in Chapter Eight, provide the foundation and critical thinking skills young people need to navigate the dangerous but predictable messages of Black popular culture and Hip Hop.

## Becoming a Cultural Worker

When I made the decision to become an academic researcher, I knew that I would research youth and Hip Hop. However, it was not until I read cultural studies theorists (e.g., Stuart Hall, Michael Eric Dyson, Cornel West, and Mark Anthony Neal), critical pedagogues (e.g., Paulo Freire, Henry Giroux), and critical feminists (e.g., Elaine Richardson, bell hooks, Patricia Hill Collins, Aisha Durham, dream hampton, and Gwendolyn D. Pough) that I understood what researching Black popular culture meant. The work of these thinkers shaped my knowledge surrounding representations and education and, ultimately, molded my worldview, similar to how Common, Jay-Z, Andre 3000, and Lauryn Hill shaped my understanding of self and community as an urban youth. Reflecting back, my initial thought was to research how youth negotiate meaning within Hip Hop music and culture through the instruction of critical pedagogy. Before I was introduced to hooks and Freire, as a teacher, I was convinced that the learning that took place in schools trumped all other sites of education—again forgetting my past. However, HCC and the above scholars complicated this notion. As I interacted with the youth of HCC and started my doctoral program, I began to understand how the community center was as vital a site of education to the students as school, if not more so. However, three concepts were missing at the center and, most important, missing from current school curricula that are crucial for students' cultural, psychological, educational, and societal success: culturally relevant pedagogy, critical and Hip Hop pedagogy, and critical media literacy. I wholeheartedly and empirically believe in the success of these three educational approaches as teaching methods that can empower students, because, in the words of Giroux (1988), "knowledge has to be meaningful to students before it can be critical" (p. 14). In today's standardized test-driven school culture, meaningful education that connects students to their community and teaches students how to investigate critically the social problems that impact their lives is missing from classrooms. Leard and Lashua (2006) state that "critical pedagogy provides a way of seeing unjust social order and revealing how this injustice has caused problems in the lives of young people who live in impoverished conditions" (p. 246). The conceptual framework of critical pedagogy provides a lens to deconstruct and make meaning of the everyday practices of youth who, in my research, interact with rap music as a site of learning.

The goal of critical pedagogy is to produce work that focuses on "the representation of texts and the construction of student subjectivity" (McLaren, 1995, p. 185). Of course, there are small pockets of educators who engage students in critical dialogue but not enough. Critical pedagogy studies that embrace Hip Hop as a pedagogical medium, called critical Hip Hop pedagogy, invoke powerful examples of youth engagement through teaching methods that help students reflect on and theorize about the music they consume. This engagement helps them meet or surpass educational goals by deconstructing the representations of Hip Hop within popular culture (Desai, 2010; Fisher, 2007; Leard & Lashua, 2006; Mahiri, 1998, 2000; Mahiri & Conner, 2003; Morrell & Duncan-Andrade, 2002; Stovall, 2006; Viola, 2003). Furthermore, Hip Hop critical pedagogy is rooted in the principles of culturally relevant pedagogy (Gay, 2000; Ladson-Billings, 1994), critical pedagogical frameworks

(Freire, 2000; Kincheloe, 2008; Shor, 1987), and cultural modeling methods (Lee, 1995). Drawing on these principles, Hip Hop critical pedagogy positions the culture, social context, learning styles, and experiences of students at the center of the curricula (Petchaur, 2009). Such culturally relevant pedagogy that utilizes Hip Hop as its framework encourages youth to engage in thoughtful discourse and meaningful classroom work that helps students connect their culture to their world. Christopher Emdin's (2010a) *Urban Science Education for the Hip-Hop Generation* and Bronwen Low's (2011) *Slam School: Learning Through Conflict in the Hip-Hop and Spoken Word Classroom* are two extraordinary examples of culturally relevant pedagogy being utilized in the classroom. These critical approaches engage students in free-thinking activities like poetry slams and innovative science lessons that draw on the life experiences of urban youth, as Hip Hoppers, and create a space for meaningful dialogue centered on the language and culture of urban students. These studies add depth and complexity to the text of Hip Hop culture and music as a site of education, with the pedagogical possibilities of individual agency, resistance, and the literacy practices of youth. These studies strengthen the rationale for using Hip Hop, critical, and culturally relevant pedagogy in urban classrooms. However, in my experience, educators who are engaging students in critical, Hip Hop, or culturally relevant pedagogy are uncommon, so many students are left to ponder the manufactured message of rap on their own. That is why academic investigations like this one are needed to document youth's understanding when educators fail to connect students' lived experiences with Hip Hop, or any other cultural phenomena, to critical pedagogy. I argue throughout this book that Black girls are engaging in critiques of rap and negotiating and attempting to overcome hegemonic conceptions of Black womanhood without any help from school officials. Black girls possess Hip Hop literacies but cannot do the work of deconstructing systemic racism; sexism; and political, social, and economic inequalities alone even though they are to some degree permanent entities within society.

In preparing myself for this project, I turned to the work of Dimitriadis (1999, 2001, 2003), Hill (2009), and Alim (2004), who all approached researching youth and Hip Hop through anthropological perspectives that recognize the ways in which youth construct meaning in their communities. Dimitriadis's 2003 book, *Friendships, Cliques, and Gangs: Young Black Men Coming of Age in Urban America,* examines how young people in a community center in a small Midwest city used popular texts to "construct, sustain, and maintain notions of self, history, and community through popular culture" (p.

6). Dimitriadis contends that an analysis of Hip Hop is important to the fields of education and cultural studies because popular culture is a site that educates us about others and about ourselves. Dimitriadis argues that too often we fail to realize that youth come to understand "notions of self and community outside of school" (2003, p. x). Dimitriadis (2001) too held several different positions at the community center where he conducted his research: mentor, tutor, staff member, and researcher.

Alim's work blends quantitative sociolinguistic analysis and ethnography to uncover the cultural practices of youth at Sunnyside Community Center in California, where he is a teacher and resident. As Alim documents how African American youth consume rap and linguistically styleshift, he also reveals how African American youth racialized gentrification and feelings of being displaced and economically disenfranchised. Hill's work, *Beats, Rhymes, and Classroom Life,* is an applied eighteen-month ethnographic study in which Hill co-taught an English literature class in an urban alternative high school in Philadelphia, Pennsylvania. Hill's work expands upon the scholarship of Hip Hop Studies and culturally relevant teaching by adding empirical data that provide insight into how youth formally and informally utilize Hip Hop as an educational process to define and redefine urban life. His work illuminates how students' surroundings impact their understanding of Hip Hop music and culture. Like Alim, Dimitriadis, and me, Hill also has multiple roles within his research site. Hill struggles with his roles as teacher-researcher and mentor-friend. The work of Alim, Dimitriadis, and Hill helps to fill an important gap within the field of Hip Hop Studies even though more research that rests on anthropological perspectives is needed.

Hip Hop scholarship formally entered the academy in 1993 with the work of Houston A. Baker, Jr., entitled *Black Studies, Rap, and the Academy.* Baker argued that the study of rap music was central to Black studies because rap was and is an "expert witness" to understanding the lives of Black urban youth. In 1994, the ground-breaking work of Tricia Rose emerged as the first ethnographic study of rap music. Her book, *Black Noise: Rap Music and Black Culture in Contemporary America,* is the foundational text for the study of Hip Hop music and culture. Rose contextualized the complexities of Hip Hop culture as it came of age in a New York City infested with economic and social inequalities. Currently, the field of Hip Hop Studies is a vast testament to how scholars wrestle with the pain and pleasure of Hip Hop as a form of Black popular culture. Hip Hop scholars' critiques have given the field insight into youth culture and how youth engage with the music. However, much of this work is theoretical.

This book responds to the lack of qualitative research on urban youth and Hip Hop, particularly urban Black females who have been pushed to the margins of society, educational research, and inner-city classrooms. Thus, the primary goal of this book is to contextualize how six Southern Black girls constructed meaning of themselves within the Hip Hop community, influenced indirectly and directly by Atlanta's political, economical, racial, and sexist milieu.

## Research, Hip Hop, and Black Girlhood

> It is only through the way in which we represent and imagine ourselves that we come to know how we are constituted and who we are.
>
> —Stuart Hall (1997, p. 30)

A common argument states that popular culture originates from working class people as an oppositional culture. However, there is a fallacy here, because the dominant group determines popular culture through the establishment of "social practices and representations that *affirm* the central values, interests, and concerns of the social class in control of the material and symbolic wealth of society" (McLaren, 1994, p. 179). Nonetheless, subcultures do emerge from the grip of the dominant group to create "space" for counterculture ideologies, such as Hip Hop in its infancy. Neal (1997) suggested that "Hip Hop perhaps represents the last black popular form to be wholly derived from the experiences and texts of the black urban landscape" (p. 128). Subsequently, contemporary rap music has fallen under the constraints of corporate America and the dominant group, much like all other forms of Black expressive culture (i.e., jazz, rhythm and blues, and soul music):

> But like Soul music a generation earlier, Hip-Hop was essentialized and sold as the "authentic" distillation of contemporary "Blackness," though in fact the form rendered "Blackness" as postmodern as Hip-Hop was itself and thus as difficult to essentialize, though its value as a mass commodity was predicated on consumer acceptance that Hip-Hop represented essential "Blackness" that was urban, youthful, and threatening.
>
> (Neal, 1997, p. 130)

The dominant group successfully folded the subculture into its ideological agenda or "superstructure" (Storey, 1998, p. 102) by commodifying "Blackness" and Hip Hop through contrived representations of cultural authenticity.

For example, numerous studies have demonstrated the ways television news programs portray Blacks as aggressive, violent, or criminal (Hansen & Hansen, 2000; Hurwitz & Peffley, 1997; Huston, Wartella, & Donnerstein, 1998). Oliver (1994) examined "reality-based" television shows and concluded that this genre over-represents violent crimes and disproportionately depicts Blacks and Latinos as criminals. Furthermore, Rideout, Lauricella, and Wartella (2011) found that on average Black and Hispanic youth spend 13 hours daily consuming media content. That time is a part of their learning experience and how they come to know and understand people who look like them and those who do not. This book is about both. The girls in this study utilized Hip Hop as one of their many mental starting points, along with conservative politics, economics, and the racial and class trends of Atlanta, to conceptualize issues surrounding race, class, sexuality, and gender. However, there is limited research investigating how young urban girls, no matter their race, construct meaning as members of the Hip Hop community.

Before the year 2000, many of the empirical studies that investigated the media centered on the impact of media violence and gender representations (Goodall, 1994; Roberts, 1991, 1994; Rose, 1991, 1994). In the fields of Hip Hop Studies and culture studies, scholarship rarely addressed how youth made meaning of Hip Hop music and culture outside of the violence represented in rap videos. Scholars within the field also failed to sit down with youth, the individuals most closely engaged with the music and culture, and ask them how they were making meaning of the representations within rap. In 1997, DuRant et al. examined the portrayal of violence and weapon carrying in music videos. The researchers reviewed 518 videos that spanned five genres (rock, rap, adult contemporary, rhythm and blues, and country and western), and their findings were consistent with much of the data that suggested that rap videos were more violent than other genres (Gerbner et al., 1994; Gow, 1999; Ward, 2004). Researchers widely agreed that rap videos were violent; however, the researchers did not interrogate the ways in which youth made meaning of rap videos in regards to race, sexuality, gender, and class. Before the start of the new decade, there was a vast amount of research that examined how youth conceptualized daytime soap operas and primetime dramas (Lowry, Love, & Kirby, 1981; Ward, 2004). Thus, researchers saw the need for studies that investigated the impact music videos had on youth, especially rap videos.

More salient for this book, research that examined Black girls' engagement with rap music and culture emerged in 2003 with Wingood et al.'s "A Prospective Study of Exposure to Rap Music Videos and African American Female

Adolescents' Health," which examined whether 522 Black girls' exposure to rap music videos could predict the high-risk behavior of young Black girls ages fourteen to eighteen. The researchers defined high-risk behavior as fighting, being arrested, using alcohol or drugs, and having multiple sex partners. The findings in this study do not show a direct correlation between exposure to rap videos and high-risk behavior; however, the results do indicate that the more teens interact with rap, the greater the risk. In 2004, Keyes examined Black female identity by interviewing Black female rappers, audience members, and music critics. Through her work, Keyes identified four categories of Black female identity within rap: Queen Mother, Fly Girls, Sista with Attitude, and Lesbian. Keyes argued that rap music provided a space for Black female rappers to make choices about their identity. However, since 2003 several researchers have conducted studies that examine how Black youth make meaning of rap videos with emphasis on the body, Black negotiations of womanhood, stereotypes, signifiers of Blackness, and Black aesthetics (Emerson, 2002; Richardson, 2007; Stephens & Few, 2007b; Stephens & Phillips, 2005; Ward, 2004; Ward, Hansbrough, & Walker, 2005). These studies all concluded that constant exposure to rap videos impacts not only the lived experiences of youth but also how they view women of color. Popular culture constructions of Black womanhood have had a profound impact on how Black women and girls view themselves (Longmore, 1998; Stephens & Few, 2007a; Stephens & Phillips, 2005; Wheeler & Petty, 2001). Stephens and Phillips's (2005) analysis of representations of Black women juxtaposed with their White counterparts in the media and within Hip Hop is worth quoting at length.

> Differentiating African American adolescent women's sexuality from white women's reinforces their positions as individuals standing on the margins of society, clarifying its boundaries (Collins, 2000; hooks and Manning, 2000). This socially constructed image of white womanhood further relies on the continued production of the racist/sexist myth that African American women are not and do not have the capacity to be sexually innocent. (p. 4)

In interrogating the issues raised by Stephens and Phillips, I think it is critical that research in the field of Hip Hop Studies begins to focus on the lives of Black girls, as Black girls' lives are linked to equalities. According to Collins (2000), Black girls have little protection from social, political, and economic injustices. This is why it is fundamental to interrogate Black girlhood. Black girls have to negotiate and navigate not only communities raided by crime, sexual assault and harassment, and poor schools but also the liberating, counter-cultural, misogynist, and sexist genre of Hip Hop music and culture, which is empowering and disempowering within the same beat. In 2007, Elaine Richardson explored the ways in which Black women negotiated stereotypical images located in rap videos. Similar to the findings within this study, Richardson found that young Black women resisted, negotiated, and succumbed to the racist stereotypes embedded in rap music and culture. Nicole Ruth Brown (2008) leads the field in Black girlhood studies with *Black Girlhood Celebration*, which is a unique examination of Black girls' relationship to Hip Hop through real-world and empirical data and celebrates Black girlhood in the contradictory culture of Hip Hop from the framework of Hip Hop feminist pedagogy. While my own book interrogates Black girls' relationship to Hip Hop music and culture, primarily rap videos, it is not a celebration, though I still wish it were. Instead, this book is a snapshot of how six Black girls understand rap music without intervention or pedagogy from school officials or myself, an approach which could assist educators in facilitating how Black girls deconstruct and recall inequality as well as moments of self-agency. Thus, the goal of this book is to unpack how six young African American girls conceptualized Hip Hop's myths about Black women within rap in conjunction with frameworks of body, signifiers of Blackness, Black womanhood, desirability, politics, and the city of Atlanta, Georgia as their vantage point. This book also looks at these frameworks in relation to myself, as I stood in their shoes in a different time and space. In no way does this book essentialize Black girls in Atlanta or Black girls anywhere. However, this work does represent some of the many ways in which Black girls, including myself, see the world, as we learn from our multiple positionalities and environments while being directly and indirectly influenced by Black popular culture and the places we reside.

# *Chapter Three*

# The New South: Gone with the Beat

> Atlanta is in many ways a paradigmatic of this ageographic and generic urbanism. Its twenty-county metropolitan area encompasses a polynucleated sprawl of sylvan suburbs, slums, and shopping malls surrounding a central archipelago of fortified fantasy islands rising out of the sea of parking lots—the whole tenuously linked by expressways, television, and a fragile sense of imagined *communitas*. As such, it provides a fertile ground for investigating the play of culture, power, identity, and place within a 'nonplace' urban realm.
>
> —Charles Rutheiser (1996, p. 4)

## "A City Too Busy to Hate" or Critique

At first glance, Atlanta is a unique Southern city: it is racially diverse, has a flourishing Black and White middle class, outstanding universities, and world-class hospitals; and, during the late '90s into the early 2000s, it was the global locus for much of rap music and popular culture. Atlanta's story of oppression and triumph seems reminiscent of something out of a fairy tale, with Atlanta as a modern-day Cinderella. However, the city has an arduous history of evil siblings: White supremacy, racism, crime, poverty, troubled public schools, and violence. Much like the outcast Cinderella, Atlanta found its glass slipper and for a moment in history escaped its dreadful past by meeting a handsome, rich prince in the form of the 1996 Olympic Games. Georgia's rush for Olympic gold created 83,000 new jobs and more than $200 million in tax revenue for the state (Rutheiser, 1996). On the surface, it would seem that the Olympic Games removed Atlanta's black cloud. Former Atlanta mayor Andrew Young shouted from the rooftops that the city's successful Olympic Games bid had "divine potential" and added "that Atlanta could play a special role in the plan of God" (Rutheiser, 1996, p. 43). With "God" on the city's side, according to

Young, everyone expected a happily-ever-after; however, this moment is when the story starts to unravel.

The city once called the "Black Mecca" by W. E. B. Du Bois for its substantial affluent Black middle class is "actually one of the poorest and most racially segregated central cities in the United States" (Rutheiser, 1996, p. 3). However, to the naked eye Atlanta's tribulations are put out of sight by "a city too busy to hate" (Hein, 1972, p. 205). The creators of the New South—a name President Kennedy gave Atlanta after the city started to "successfully" desegregate schools—deliberately engineered a metropolis that appeared on the surface to be politically liberal and economically sound. Thus, it served as living proof of its native son, Dr. Martin Luther King, Jr.'s, dream for racial harmony. As such, Atlanta is a complex city, still trying to run away from its past of hate, segregation, White flight, Southern conservatism, racism, and sexism by masking it with a new conservative ideology of color-blindness and underpinnings of individual rights, privatization, and free market enterprise (Kruse, 2007). Atlanta has a unique and unparalleled social and political history and serves as the vantage point for this book.

As stated in Chapter Two, there is a dire need for ethnographic studies that examine the lives of African American urban girls, specifically by scholars who understand the social and historical context of their daily existence. With context being such an essential ingredient of this book, the study's research location of Atlanta, Georgia, is as much a part of this book as the experiences of Lara, Nicole, Lisa, Star, Maxine, and Dee. For these six girls, Atlanta is home. A discussion regarding Atlanta is incomplete without the mention of racial inequality, Jim Crow, Dr. Martin Luther King, Jr., the Civil Rights Movement, soul and gospel music, Black megachurches, the Southern Christian Leadership Conference, Sweet Auburn Avenue, Jack the Rapper, Ryan Cameron, Frank Ski, Ted Turner, gay pride, the 1996 Olympic Games, Morehouse and Spelman Colleges, Coca-Cola, Black radio, Jazz Funk Kafe, LaFace Records, Freaknik, gratification, strip clubs, and Southern-flavored Hip Hop music and culture (this list is in no way exhaustive). These items may seem unrelated at first glance, but when interlocked they create the backdrop for the Southern "urban girl story" (Evans-Winters, 2005). The purpose of this chapter is to examine how the research location, social and racial inequalities, conservatism, and the rise of Southern Hip Hop all influenced the outcome of this book, myself, and my participants.

## Taking the Soul out of a City: G-Town

Disclosing one's research location is risky, especially within qualitative research. However, in order to fully understand the home environment of these six girls, a historical and social examination of Atlanta is necessary. Just under a half million people live in Atlanta, and 56 percent of the population is Black. Atlanta is what many refer to as a "chocolate city," where Black folks outnumber the White population, with a native-born Black middle class (Rutheiser, 1996). Over the years, Atlanta's Black leadership has emerged from the pulpits, the Civil Rights Movement, and purposefully homegrown Black professionals who have changed and continue to change the trajectory of Atlanta and U.S. politics. The city has had a string of Black Democratic mayors since 1973, beginning with Maynard H. Jackson, Jr., who was the first Black mayor of a major Southern city. His election symbolized a shift in power from the White establishment and illustrated the gains of the Civil Rights Movement in the South. However, Whites rejected the New South and retaliated by fleeing to the suburbs—a phenomenon sociologists referred to as White Flight. According to Kruse (2007), White Flight arose from Whites' belief that, "Atlanta 'belonged' to them as racial birthright" (p. 125). Thus, their move to suburbia was part of a massive resistance that created a racial environmental barrier between Black and White Atlantans in the New South.

Despite the enormous political victories of the Civil Rights Movement, with the aftermath of slavery—Jim Crow—and the Supreme Court's ruling against school segregation in the landmark case *Brown v. Board of Education*, Atlanta still carried with it a caste system for Blacks, which, in turn, produced an uphill battle for Black leadership, both locally and nationally. Although Blacks had political power as the face of the mayoral position, Whites still controlled Atlanta as they resisted desegregation and Black leadership (Kruse, 2007; Rutheiser, 1996). Therefore, the social and economic advancements of Black folks could not compete with the profound and insidious legacy of White supremacy and racism. Even though the election of Black mayors brought new possibilities for the Black community, with many Black-owned firms awarded public-sector contracts, Atlanta was nationally known for its high crime rate. James Baldwin (1985) referred to Atlanta as "a kind of grotesque Disneyland" (p. 1). Between 1965 and 1970, Atlanta was the country's murder capital. Between 1979 and 1987, twenty-eight Black children were murdered. These cases were known as the Atlanta Child Murders. Wayne Williams, a young Black man, was found guilty of the murders; however, much of the evidence was circumstantial. In 1993, Williams's lawyer argued for a new trial after learning that police and prosecutors suppressed evidence, which included tapes of Ku Klux Klan members confessing to a number of the murders (Kruse, 2007, p. 104). According to Kruse, allegations that the Klan was responsible for some of the killings were ignored by mainstream Atlanta news outlets. Atlanta's leaders did not want the city's dirty laundry aired and therefore fought to suppress any information that highlighted Atlanta's racial divide.

The city's segregationist state of mind led to the discriminatory policies of *de facto* and *de jure* segregation, which resulted in the racial inequalities of opportunities for wealth, homeownership, inheritance, and adequate education (Oliver & Shapiro, 1997; Shapiro, 2004). Sadly, the racism that built Atlanta and much of the South is still present today. However, the message has changed. It has become more subtly coded in language. For example, in 1994 when former Speaker of the House Newt Gingrich spoke to Cobb County reporter Peter Applebone, he stated, "The people want safety, and they believe big cities have failed and are controlled by people who are incapable of delivering goods and services" (quoted in Kruse, 2007, p. 260). Gingrich went on to add that

> [w]hat people worry about is the bus line gradually destroying one apartment complex after another, bringing people out of public housing who have no middle class values and whose kids as they become teenagers often are centers of robbery and where the schools collapse because the parents that live in the apartment complexes don't care that kids don't do well in school and the whole school collapses.
>
> (quoted in Kruse, 2007, p. 261)

Gingrich's words explicitly represent the thoughts and feelings of many White Atlantans and fuel the suburban Sunbelt conservative epistemology and movement, which also extends to the current Tea Party movement. As I walked the streets and rode the MARTA (Atlanta's public transportation system) through the neighborhoods and apartment complexes that Gingrich portrayed—where my own mother lives—I found individuals shut out by a city built to keep people of color isolated and detached from Atlanta's so-called progressive mantra. This paradoxical situation is not surprising in a city heavily populated by Black folks with Black leadership but based on a provocative past of segregation, forced desegregation, and wealthy White Atlantans made wealthy by the hands of Blacks.

For the purposes of this book, I will refer to the Atlanta neighborhood surrounding the community center as G-town. I purposefully named this vicinity G-town because of the gentrification that took place during the time I spent working and researching in the neighborhood. When I first took the job at HCC, I rode two buses and a train to get to work every day. If I drove to work it would have taken at most fifteen minutes. Although my journey on public transportation was a ninety-minute ordeal, traveling from downtown Atlanta to G-town became a daily informal research project. I observed twenty-first-century gentrification stemming from neoliberal urbanism, which emphasizes the privatization of inner-city lands and housing markets with the intent of restructuring urban areas for mixed income living. Gentrification functions as a social and economical process that typically displaces working class residents and people of color. As the middle class moves into areas once occupied by the working poor, the property values skyrocket and subsequently price the previous residents out of the market. Gentrification is a discrete and hegemonic force that rearticulates urban discourse and the racial composition of urban areas. Developers redefine words and phrases like *urban*, *in-town living*, *mixed income*, and *live, work, play communities* to appeal to members of the White middle class who are now abandoning the white picket fences of the suburbs and moving to rehabbed urban areas of color for a gaze into urban culture, convenience, and the possibility of a high return upon selling their homes in the future. Supposedly, an influx of White middle class residents will decrease crime, enhance schools, and diversify the community for the better. The developers and city officials sell the venture as a win-win partnership for all parties involved. Across America, gentrification has become a popular fix for financially struggling inner cities like Atlanta. Furthermore, gentrification among young White, middle class liberals is seen as trendy. In the book *Stuff White People Like: A Definitive Guide to the Unique Taste of Millions*, gentrification is number 73 out of 150 things White people use to establish a White racial identity. When writing about gentrification, Christian Lander (2008) states, "White people like to live in these neighborhoods [Black and Brown communities] because they get credibility and respect from other white people for living in a more 'authentic' neighborhood where they are exposed to 'true culture' every day" (p. 91). Although the book is written in an upbeat and jovial manner, it captures how poor communities are stripped of their culture as a result of gentrification, which displaces community members and causes the community's activities and traditions to disappear.

In March of 2006, the *New York Times* published an article highlighting the fact that, for the first time since the 1920s, Atlanta's Black population was declining and its White occupancy rate was steadily increasing. This flux has influenced the city's longstanding Black leadership as fewer Blacks are turning out to vote. For example, in the Old Fourth Ward where Dr. Martin Luther King, Jr. was born, 19 percent of the community's Black residents have fled due to the replacement of low-rent apartments with pricey upscale developments (Dewan, 2006). The historic district that was once 94 percent Black is now down to 74 percent and is steadily becoming Whiter. In 2009, Atlanta's mayoral race resulted in a runoff between Republican Mary Norwood, the city's first potential White mayor in thirty-six years, and her Black opponent, State Senator Kasim Reed. The new racial makeup of the city played a major part in Norwood's campaign for mayor. According to the Brookings Institution, between 2000 and 2006 Atlanta's White population grew faster than that of any other U.S. city (Gurwitt, 2008). Ultimately, Reed won the election; however, Norwood won the White, Republican, and Independent votes by a six-to-one margin (Goddard, 2009). Going into the election, she was seen as the frontrunner. Reed's slim victory by only 714 votes (Suggs & Stirgus, 2009) is an indication of elections to come. Looking at Atlanta within a larger context, Norwood's popularity with White Republican voters upholds a longstanding tradition of Georgia as a conservative Republican state.

Although present-day Atlanta is considered a liberal city with a substantial queer population, its Southern roots of segregation, inequality, racism, and White privilege still lurk within the red hills of Georgia. In one telling example, during an interview with a local ABC affiliate in Atlanta, a young blonde woman told a reporter that if Norwood was elected, "Atlanta won't be known as A-T-L anymore. Won't be known as the place where rappers are. We'll have a clean safe city where white people can relate to" (YouTube, November 3, 2009). City officials and news media argued that race was not a factor in Atlanta's mayoral runoff after the election of Obama and post-racial politics. However, although he did garner a substantial 42 percent of the White vote, Obama did not win the White vote in the presidential election (Wise, 2009). In fact, John McCain won the Electoral College votes in Georgia. During my five years as an Atlanta resident, it was easy to forget that Atlanta is merely a Democratic island in the conservative red state of Georgia. As illustrated by the interviewee's comments above, the rest of the state often sees Atlanta through its Dirty South music and its global Black identity.

However, before rap was Atlanta's musical and cultural canvas and before the Olympic torch was carried through the city's streets, Atlanta was known to many African Americans for its historically Black colleges and annual Black college Spring Break mega party known as "Freaknic." Freaknic was an invasion of Black bodies in "public" spaces often regarded as White areas of the city. The spring break celebration earned its name from the popular 1970s songs "The Freak" by the group Chic and "Freak of the Week" by Funkadelic (Thompson, 2007). Joined with the communal practice of picnicking, the festival established "racially charged conflicts between and among the city's African-American political establishment, the media, and an urban population divided not only by race, but by class, generation, and lifestyle" (Rutheiser, 1996, p. 133). The legacy of Freaknic is as much a part of Atlanta's regional identity as rap and Coca-Cola.

## Southern Hospitality—Freaknic Style

In 1982, Black college students from the United States, Canada, and the Caribbean took to the streets of Atlanta for a three-day weekend reminiscent of New Orleans's Mardi Gras and Trinidad's annual Carnival celebrations. What differentiated Freaknic from a yearly street festival was the region. The Dirty South's bass-driven music, sexually explicit lyrics, and young Black females' willingness to perform erotically for their male counterparts gave the city what the *Atlanta Journal Constitution* called "Freaknikaphobia" (quoted in Thompson, 2007, p. 25). Freaknic was a twenty-four-hour mobile strip club–rap video in the boulevards and avenues of Atlanta. Black women would give impromptu striptease-like dances on top of cars or in the middle of the street while males captured every promiscuous move with a video camera. Any male with a camcorder became a video director. According to Thompson (2007), women of color's participation at Freaknic was "driven by the desire to be seen and, perhaps more importantly, to be photographed and videotaped . . . men were photographic shooters on the hunt for female performers" (p. 30). Thus, what started out as a local gathering of a couple hundred Black students from Morehouse and Spelman Colleges grew over a twelve-year span to become the city's number one enemy in the early 1990s and came to a head just prior to the 1996 Olympic Games. The local media and White Atlantans proclaimed that Freaknic was a "takeover" of the city by Black youth. By 1994 over 200,000 people participated, convening in Atlanta's upscale Piedmont Park.

As Freaknic's attendance multiplied, it divided the city residents by color: "69% of African American residents thought Freaknic was good for the city, while 62% of White[s] considered the event harmful, and cited traffic, sexual harassment and looting as problems" (Meyers, 2004, p. 102). Local government officials, most notably the city's mayor, Bill Campbell, were strong-armed by White constituents to act. Atlanta's news coverage demonized the spring break partakers as lewd underclass troublemakers unaccustomed to middle class values and norms (Meyers, 2004). The racial undertones were highlighted by Atlanta's Black community members, who drew comparisons of Freaknic to Atlanta's annual gay pride parade, which at the time was also held in Piedmont Park and generated a great deal of nudity (Thompson, 2007). The city's Blackness was on display for all to see, which resulted in much public pressure on city officials and Mayor Campbell. In 1995, a year before the Olympic Games, Campbell declared an end to Freaknic by establishing laws that made it almost impossible for promoters to hold an event on public property. For example, promoters seeking to have an event in a local park needed a million-dollar insurance policy and the approval of a fifteen-member city-appointed board (Thompson, 2007). Also, police discouraged Freaknickers with barricades, roadblocks, city curfew laws, and "red-lining" to redirect Freaknic traffic out of White neighborhoods and into Black neighborhoods (Thompson, 2007; Meyers, 2004). Black voters viewed Mayor Campbell's anti-Freaknic position as a calculated political maneuver to appease his "White constituents in the racially polarized city" (Thompson, 2007, p. 39). As Meyers (2004) points out, the city's management of the issue "reeked of racism" (p. 111).

However, more than racism was at play within the space of Freaknic. The media coverage and overall comments regarding the event illustrate how race, class, and gender intersect. Atlanta's local media portrayed Black females as "stereotypic Jezebels" who were deserving of sexual violence because their acts did not align with White Atlantans' norms (Meyers, 2004). Gilroy (1994) argues that Blacks' struggles for freedom manifest via the sexualization and concentration on the body, which he calls "bio-politics" (p. 25). Furthermore, Lipsitz (1994) adds that Hip Hop and African American youth culture are countercultural social norms. Lipsitz suggests that "bodies, ghetto walls, and city streets" are "sites of performance and play," as youth of color disrupt and respond to oppression (p. 21). Freaknickers were viewed by Atlantans as the "ultimate outsiders" (Alexander, 1995, p. 15) due to their race, class, and gender. Freaknic's popularity diminished as society's "cultural surveillance" (Lipsitz, 1994, p. 21) of Black bodies increased, and government officials sanctioned the event with laws that profiled Blacks. Consequently, the end of Freaknic marked the rise of Southern-flavored Hip Hop with Atlanta as its bedrock.

## U.S.A. (United States of Atlanta)

> Whether you're from the South Bronx, South Central L.A., or South Dakota, the South is part of us all.
>
> —Roni Sarig (2007, p. xx)

> Most explicitly, the rise of Atlanta's "Dirty South" rap music industry shows the readiness of some African Americans in the post-civil rights era not only to embrace their southerness but to sell it as well.
>
> —Darren Grem (2006, p. 56)

There is something infectious about Southern rap, especially the ATL's Dirty South rap style. It seems to have all the right ingredients. The Southern rap spirit has soul, passion, rhythm, warmth, funk, youthfulness, and, most important, heart. Heart is slang for someone who overcomes adversity no matter the circumstances. Southern rap seems effortless and forceful at the same time. Atlanta's special brand of Southern rap style is grounded in the sounds that came before rap: West African storytellers (griots), spoken word, slave songs coded in metaphors and euphemisms, spirituals, the African drum, bebop, call and response, blues, jazz, funk, rhythm and blues, soul, rock and roll, and Civil Rights freedom songs (Sarig, 2007; McBride, 2007). The eclectic historical nature of Southern rap explains its pervasiveness. Hip Hop encompasses almost all genres of music, and Southern Hip Hop is the "genesis of rap" (Sarig, 2007, p. xii). Roni Sarig (2007), author of the book *Third Coast: OutKast, Timbaland, and How Hip-Hop Became a Southern Thing*, suggests that "rap music was born in the South" and that "[t]he rise of Southern hip-hop, then, represents the first large-scale break from New York's dominance" (p. xv). What differentiates Southern rap from West and East Coast rap is that it speaks directly through a Southern drawl that expresses the pain of enduring slavery, racial inequality, the joy and pride of being Black, and the unwavering spirituality of Black folks.

Atlanta's musical dominance within urban culture is not new; it has been a burgeoning phenomenon since 1949 when Atlanta became home to the nation's first Black-owned and -operated radio station, WERD 1160 AM (Barlow, 1999). Radio jockey Jack Gibson, one of the most popular Black radio personalities of his era, became the voice of WERD in its Sweet Auburn Avenue studio. Gibson was well known and respected throughout Black radio. He partied with Thurgood Marshall, handed his microphone to Dr. Martin Luther King, Jr., and broadcast from Miami's only Black hotel with Nat King Cole, Sarah Vaughan, and Sammy Davis, Jr. (Barlow, 1999; Sarig, 2007). His charismatic personality landed him the nickname Jack the Rapper for "tellin' it like T-I-S is" (Sarig, 2007, p. 96). After leaving radio, but not the entertainment business, Gibson and his wife, Sayde, utilized their fame and influence to spearhead Atlanta's first Black music convention in 1977, entitled "Jack the Rapper's First Family Affair." Mayor Maynard Jackson supported the event, which occurred annually until 1994 and competed with Freaknic for attendants. Gibson's Family Affair put Atlanta on top of the urban music food chain as the "capital of urban music" (Sarig, 2007, p. 97). Acts like Clarence Carter, Curtis Mayfield, and the S.O.S Band called Atlanta home, and James Brown was just a few miles away in Augusta, Georgia.

Although R&B and soul music reigned supreme, rap was on its heels with the Sugarhill Gang's 1979 hit, "Rapper's Delight." This one song singlehandedly caused record companies to reevaluate the mass appeal of rap to mainstream consumers. Critics believed rap would go the way of disco and fade over time (George, 1999). However, rap's authentic sound resonated with youth across America. In the '80s and early '90s, New York City was the Mecca of rap and home to the originators of Hip Hop culture. Meanwhile, major Southern rap artists were busy putting their cities on the map by crafting a Southern style of rap music heavily influenced by sexually charged rappers Luke Campbell and 2 Live Crew (Miami), and the urban tales of D.O.C., Ghetto Boys (Houston), Eightball, Pretty Tony (Memphis), and Master P (New Orleans). In Atlanta, local groups such as Succes-N-Effect, Kilo, and Tag Team were receiving national attention. Tag Team was best known for their 1993 chart-topping hit "Whoomp (There It Is)," which took the thirty-ninth spot on *Billboard*'s Top 200. Subsequently, Atlanta natives like Jermaine Dupri, Dallas Austin, and OutKast members Andre Benjamin and Antwan "Big Boi" Patton were listening, watching, and developing their own sound unique to the ATL. At the core of Atlanta's musical success were record moguls and song writers Antonio "L.A." Reid and Kenneth "Babyface" Edmonds, who established

Atlanta as the "Motown of the South" with LaFace Records (Sarig, 2007). LaFace's acts included TLC, Usher, and Toni Braxton, who all had crossover appeal and topped the *Billboard* charts. Later, OutKast and Goodie Mob would also sign with LaFace Records. In addition, Dupri's record label, So So Def (Dupri borrowed a portion of the name from legendary New York rap record label Def Jam), launched the teenage rap group Kris Kross, who in May of 1993 took the number one spot on both the Top 200 and R&B/Hip Hop *Billboard* charts. However, LaFace and So So Def's success did not sit well with the Hip Hop community outside Atlanta and the South. Although Kris Kross was a household name, the established Hip Hop community viewed the duo as a marketing gimmick (i.e., wearing their clothes backwards) and not as "real" Hip Hop artists, who mostly came out of the East or West Coast at that time.

In 1994, OutKast's first album, *Southernplayalisticcadillacmuzic*, debuted as an eclectic tapestry of sound, vivid storytelling, slick rhythms, and Southern charm. The album would climb to number three on *Billboard*'s top R&B/Hip Hop chart; however, New York was not ready to hand over the reins to the South just yet. When OutKast and Goodie Mob arrived in New York for the 1995 Source Awards, they were booed after winning Best New Rap Group. Clearly Hip Hop was not yet "southernized" (Grem, 2006). George (1999) argued that "Hip Hop America" overlooked Southern rap, particularly due to the deadly East/West Coast rivalry and the regional identity that stereotyped Southern rappers as "country" because of their Southern accents, as heard through Northern ears. According to Sarig (2007),

> [i]n the two years and one month between the release of OutKast's second album, "ATLiens," and third album, "Aquemini," hip-hop changed dramatically. Just weeks after "ATLiens" hit the charts, iconic West Coast rapper Tupac Shakur was shot and killed in Las Vegas. And five months later, his New York rival, Notorious B.I.G., died by gunfire as well. (p. 170)

OutKast's unfortunate timing would end in 2004 with the release of the six-time Grammy-winning album *Speakerboxx/The Love Below*. At that moment, mainstream and corporate America, and casual as well as die-hard rap fans, all positioned their eyes and ears on the Dirty South. With chart topper after chart topper, the rap world has not taken its hands off the purse strings of Atlanta since. A region that was once booed is now one of the front-runners in America's Hip Hop industry (Grem, 2006; Sarig, 2007).

The most telling example of Atlanta's reign over rap occurred in November of 2006 when Black Entertainment Television (BET) held its first Hip Hop Awards show at Atlanta's Fox Theater. With Atlanta natives winning eight of the seventeen awards and taking the stage for five of the ten performances, the marriage between Hip Hop and the city of Atlanta was evident. Atlanta's success within the music industry created a platform to display Southern rap and culture to folks outside of Atlanta and the South. Thus, popular culture introduced non-Southerners to the Dirty South and the Southern Black experience.

## Regional and Racial Identity of the Dirty South

At its core, in its rawest form, rap tackles the complexities of America: poverty, politics, joblessness, crime, sexism, gang activity, violence, greed, racism, and injustice. That fearlessness is how the culture of Hip Hop emerged in multi-cultural communities within the U.S. and across the globe. Although Hop Hip's contemporary roots are grounded in its birthplace, New York City, the "cross fertilization of African identities informed by Caribbean, African, Puerto-Rican, and African-American experiences" (Houston, 2008, p. 73) undergirds Hip Hop as the musical and culture embodiment of modern Black life. Ironically, such innate complexity makes Hip Hop accessible to the masses and moldable to almost any geographic location. That approachability is the reason why Hip Hop music streaming from Atlanta became so popular in the later 1990s and early 2000s. In the late 1990s, Blacks in Atlanta endured the highest levels of poverty, crime, and spatial segregation of any American metropolitan area (Rutheiser, 1996). These elements were key in driving Atlanta's Hip Hop music, but the rap industry initially dismissed Atlantans' struggles because of their locale. Southern rappers were largely ignored because many Black folks, mainly those outside of the South, viewed them as "country." Grem (2006) suggests that Blacks use the epithet "country" in a way similar to White culture's "redneck." Before OutKast, non-Southerners perceived Southern rappers as "un-urban, unsophisticated, and 'backwards'" (p. 62) and therefore incapable of producing "real" rap music. The success, sophistication, musicality, and innovative rap style of OutKast debunked the regional myths of Southern Black folks as unintelligent. Along with other Southern rap groups like Goodie Mob and Field Mob, they expressed to America and the Hip Hop community at large the real life experiences of being Black, young, and living in the post-civil rights Southern tier. Rhythms about fish 'n' grits, candy-painted

Cadillacs, pimps, and strippers dancing layered over addictive beats captivated the rap community. With OutKast at the helm, the Dirty South's music and Southern culture redefined "country" and rap music as a whole. The "country grammar" of Southern rappers became America's new addiction.

OutKast, however, was just the beginning of a major movement. By the mid-2000s, the "Southernization" of Hip Hop was in full force, with a growing number of Hip Hop artists like Ludacris, Killer Mike, Young Jeezy, Li'l Scrappy, T.I., the Ying Yang Twins, and Li'l John and the East Side Boyz topping the charts. These artists arrived on the Atlanta scene with a sound that listeners and critics considered more risqué than their predecessors' (Sarig, 2007). Atlanta's post-OutKast and Goodie Mob rap artists reinvented the sexually charged and explicit "booty shake" music that made Luke Campbell and the 2 Live Crew famous in the 1990s. They infused their music with Miami-style bass music and the beats of the African drum to form a regional sound driven by infectious beats and jaw-dropping misogynistic sexual lyrics that manifested from Atlanta's prominent, sexually driven subculture of strip clubs and adult entertainment. This subculture is also where Southern women enter rap music, not as rappers or producers but as "shake dancers" who regulate Atlanta's music by "how low they can go."

Up until this point, this chapter has focused on Atlanta Hip Hop without once mentioning how Southern females have influenced the music. However, I cannot write about what does not exist. Hip Hop is a male-dominated industry, and Hip Hop in the South is no different. Certainly Southern women have contributed to the success of Southern rap, but from the sidelines or the pole, as consumers and video vixens. There has never been a prominent female Southern rapper who is comparable to Jay-Z or T.I. Furthermore, the male domination of rap has shut out or pigeon-holed many female MCs. Some of the most successful female MCs—like Roxanne Shanté, Salt-N-Pepa, Queen Latifah, MC Lyte, Ladybug Mecca, Yo-Yo, Foxy Brown, and Li'l Kim—had careers that were short lived or evolved into actresses or vocalists. Moreover, the aforementioned female MCs are from the North, primarily New York and New Jersey, with the exception of Yo-Yo, who is from South Central, Los Angeles. Only a few Southern female MCs, like Trina, Khia, Mia X, Gangsta Boo, and Missy "Misdemeanor" Elliott, have risen above the Mason Dixon Line into the "antiwoman" space of rap (George, 1999). The only female rapper from Atlanta to have any force within rap was the late Lisa "Left Eye" Lopes of the R&B girl group TLC. In the 1990s, TLC had a stint of multimillion-dollar-selling albums. Although TLC's success spanned a decade, many rap fans do not consider Left Eye to be a true female MC because of her roots as part of a singing group. Rap scholar Nelson George (1999) suggests that rap's street origins and "macho values" make it an almost impractical space for female MCs to redefine or challenge the glass ceiling. George writes, "I would argue that if none of these female artists had ever made a record, hip hop's development would have been no different" (p. 184). Rap and femininity have a contentious partnership, where sexism flourishes and female degradation is the norm. Within Hip Hop culture, Black female sexual agency is a slippery slope that manifests easily as exploitation. Atlanta's female sexual agency is complex: Female strippers control the sounds of Southern rap by the size of their butt and the shape of their hips. Since sex is the muse behind many marketing campaigns in popular culture, rap represents the ethos of the Black adult sex industry, and in the world of Southern rap, strippers are the pulse of the music.

## How Low Can You Go?

> [Atlanta] is the city where the adult entertainment industry is second only to Coca-Cola.
>
> —Jacklyn "Diva" Bush (2003, p. 10)

> Black folks have always walked both sides of the tracks—on one praising the Lord, on the other sweating happily with the Devil.
>
> —Nelson George (1999, p.180)

In an interview with Tamara Palmer, author of *Country Fried Soul: Adventures in Dirty South Hip Hop*, Atlanta rapper I-20 explains the impact strippers have on both the local and potential national success of rap music. I-20 explains, "I'm from a city where a stripper's always been a star. . . . The strip club is huge. . . . The stripper is your first test audience if you're a local rapper" (p. 46). Here, I-20 describes the marriage between the industries of adult entertainment and Hip Hop. Both industries celebrate a hypersexual lifestyle and reap billions in yearly revenue (Miller-Young, 2008) by selling Black sexuality. Strategically structured by modern capitalism, this popularized form of Black sexuality perpetuates White supremacist patriarchy, which perceives Black women and men as untamed sexual creatures with insatiable appetites for sex (Collins, 2004; Miller-Young, 2008). The narrative that Black women and men are sexually deviant fits perfectly into the erotic personas of both industries. Moreover, it illustrates the contemporary take on the canonization of the Black female body and the sexual stereotypes that demonize Black women, as invoked by larger U.S. sexual policies of racism, sexism, exploitation, and heterosexism (Collins, 2004).

Yet, Southern Hip Hop muddles the historically subordinate position of Black female sexuality within popular culture and capitalism. In the South, female strippers are celebrated as icons of Black sexuality, beauty, and erotic prowess. And, as I-20 explains, strip clubs are the testing ground for Atlanta's Hip Hop sound. Strippers' ability to "get low" or "drop it like it's hot" to a particular song serves as an indicator of the record's likely success. According to Dupri, strippers determine if a record is ready for mass distribution: "I feel like that's the place where you can get the most spins on your records, anyway—in the strip club. If the girls like to dance off one of your songs, nine times out of ten, it's gon' be a hit record" (quoted in Palmer, 2005, p. 46). Thus, "shake dancers" in the Dirty South represent more than just booty droppin' and p-poppin'—they are the ear and pulse of Hip Hop consumers at large (Sharpley-Whiting, 2007). Strip clubs are a complex space where pornographic Black female labor operates as a market analyst that has revolutionized the commercialization of Atlanta's rap scene and the entire Dirty South (Sharpley-Whiting, 2007). For twenty dollars—a fraction of the cost of radio and street promotion—a rapper can utilize strippers as pollsters who provide anecdotal potential market success (Sharpley-Whiting, 2007). Sharpley-Whiting suggests that strip clubs are rappers' boardrooms, where deals are made while butts shake and strippers bend over and touch their toes. Rappers from every coast shout out Atlanta strip clubs and individual strippers in their songs, oftentimes thanking strippers for their Southern hospitality and launching their careers.

Strippers are the gatekeepers to Southern Hip Hop's hypersexual playground. As such, they have a complicated agency within a male-dominated industry. The voyeurism of Hip Hop and the easy accessibility of pornographic Black female labor invoke the sexism and misogyny that stand as precursors for Hip Hop's global appeal. Strippers, video vixens, and groupies are racially essentialized as hos, freaks, and Black whores (Miller-Young, 2008; Sharpley-Whiting, 2007). Strip clubs represent a section of Southern rap where Black women have autonomy, where voyeurs desire and celebrate their bodies for a shape that the dominant culture once saw as repulsive. However, the hyperexposure they receive as contemporary stereotypical sexual objects results in the sexual harassment, rape, and sexual assault of women of color (Miller-Young, 2008; Sharpley-Whiting, 2007). Although a culture that celebrates the voluptuous backsides of women of color has replaced the trope of the "Hottentot Venus," according to Sharpley-Whiting, Black women are 10 percent more likely to be victimized sexually than all other women combined, and 61 percent of sexual violence goes unreported (Sharpley-Whiting, 2007). In Sharpley-Whiting's *Pimps Up, Ho's Down: Hip Hop's Hold on Young Black Women*, she calls for the Hip Hop generation to seriously examine its role in the sexual abuse of women.

> In what ways does hip hop culture ride shotgun in a culture already rife with sexual abuse? How does this culture reinforce stereotypes of Black women as 'so hot' that they are rendered fair game for rape and sexual assault? (p. 58)

These questions underpin Hip Hop's gender politics, which openly celebrates Black female sexuality and gives women of color the power to regulate the sound of Southern rap through exotic dance, all while sexually abusing and exploiting women of color to the same audience. Atlanta's strip club culture is a play on an old trope, with nuances of female agency. Strippers' agency is limited and narrow and controlled by the male gaze, but an agency nonetheless—one permeated by capitalism. Drawing on Foucault's (1995) ideas of agency and power, social context is essential. Strippers have autonomy within the world of Southern rap because their bodies are not completely "docile" (Foucault, 1977, p. 138). For example, when strippers of color exercise calculated manipulations of their bodies, they set the standard and regulate the music of Southern rap. Within the social background of strip clubs, women of color create new notions of mainstream desirability. One can easily contend, however, that these novel identities formed by strippers reinforce the historical degradations of women of color as hypersexual women driven by financial gain. Moreover, strippers work in insulated spaces where their bodies are under constant surveillance—incapable of an emancipatory performance. In trying to unpack the muddled space of Atlanta's strip club culture, which can be simultaneously liberating and oppressive, I am in no way suggesting that female liberation can be found within the confines of booty poppin' strip clubs—but it does present a tangled web for young Black girls to reason with. In Chapter Five, I examine how young Black girls growing up in this hypersexual, racially divided, female fetish space of Atlanta's rap culture make meaning of Black and White bodies in order to determine the societal merit of women who enter the rap video industry. However, before I present my findings, I think it is important to discuss their limitations and how my multiple positionalities initially impacted my research.

## *Chapter Four*

# Starting with My Limitations: Positionality, Power, and Reflexivity

In an effort to prevent the "unseen and unforeseen dangers" (Milner, 2007) of conducting qualitative inquiry, some of the first concepts a novice qualitative researcher learns are positionality, reflexivity, and power relations. Milner argues that "unforeseen dangers are those that are unanticipated or unpredicted in the research project based on the decisions that researchers make in the research process" (p. 388). When beginning my dissertation, I embarked upon the most important and life-changing research project of my life believing that I had taken every precaution to ensure few to no unseen dangers. As a Black researcher, I entered the field aware of race-based epistemologies (Banks, 1993; Dillard, 2000; Ladson-Billings & Tate, 1995; Tyson, 1998) and culturally sensitive research approaches (Denzin & Lincoln, 1994; Dillard, 2000; Tillman, 2002). As outlined in Chapter Two, I construct meaning through the lens of Hip Hop feminism, but that is just one of my positionalities; I am also a queer researcher who approached my research at HCC through the lens of queer theory. Before entering HCC, I thought that these two frameworks and my background as an inner-city youth made me a researcher who understood Hip Hop, youth, sexuality, and what it took to research in the inner city. I was eager to examine heteronormativity, desires, and essentialist constructs (Butler, 1990; Halberstam, 2005; Warner, 1993) at HCC. Because I was current in the literature and from the "'hood," I assumed I was ready and prepared to work with inner-city young girls. I believed myself nearly immune to falling into one of Milner's "unforeseen dangers." However, there was an unseen outlier in this process: me. I had never examined my positionalities as a researcher working with Southern Black girls to realize how complex a space it would be for me. Although I read about being reflective, it did not work its way into my doctoral degree pursuit until it was too late. I found myself in the field hitting roadblocks because my personal baggage was obstructing my research and my relationship with the young women of HCC.

Through personal exploration and the help of Lara, Nicole, Star, Dee, Maxine, and Lisa, I realized that my closed-minded perception of the South caused me to assume the girls had negative attitudes and assumptions regarding queerness, which led me to internalize homophobia (Shidlo, 1994; Sophie, 1987; Szymanski & Chung, 2001). Researching in heteronormative spaces—along with my own childhood stereotypes of the South, Black Southern churches, and fear of discussing my queerness with teenage girls—ultimately impeded my research and limited my work. However, through my research I began to engage in the contradictory, complex, fluid, and unfinished space of forming my identity as an African American lesbian living in the South. I believe it is important and necessary as a qualitative researcher that I examine my positionality as a researcher within the pages of this book before presenting my data, since I am the measurement tool. I also think it is important to describe my experiences working as what I thought to be an "openly" queer researcher in Atlanta, Georgia, as my lens influenced how I interpreted, presented, and disseminated my data. With that being said, this chapter will chronicle my identity struggles as a Black lesbian, the challenges I faced, which I imposed on myself as a queer researcher, and how my views of the South were challenged and demystified by six heterosexual young Black girls who taught me something I thought I already knew: how to be open and queer in the South. If the girls did not discredit my destructive perceptions regarding them and their Southern roots, this book would not be.

## "I Am from New York, but I Got Country Cousins" —Talib Kweli

Every summer during my childhood, my family traveled to Florida to reconnect with our Southern family members. My family was like many African American families who migrated to the North from the South in search of economic prosperity. I distinctly remember the almost two-day trip from Rochester, New York, to Jacksonville, Florida, in a baby blue 1985 Cadillac Sedan de Ville, which had leather seats and power windows. To my father, this car was more than a mode of transportation: It represented to him and to his family members that he "made it," and driving it home meant everything to him. In preparation for the trip, it was my job to ensure that the interior was shiny and pearly white. My father embraced his Southern roots; he had spent his adolescence in Jacksonville. On the other hand, my mother was born and raised in upstate New York. She considered herself a Black woman from Rochester, and Black folks below the Mason Dixon line were "country." Ironically, my maternal grandmother is from Conway, South Carolina, one of the oldest cities in the state. Growing up, even with my Southern kinships, I believed that many Southerners were uneducated and unrefined because of the way they spoke or where they lived. Even as I spent the summers with my Southern relatives, I was indirectly led to believe that I was "better" than my Southern counterparts. It was not only my mother who professed that Black folks from the South were inferior—the message was explicit in my community. As a member of the Hip Hop generation who situates aspects of my cultural identity within the music and culture of Hip Hop—I fervently embraced early Hip Hop's regional dominance, which proclaimed that New York City was the center of rap and proliferated the stereotype that Southern rappers were "country."

My experience growing up urban, Northern, and a lover of Hip Hop music and culture shaped my views of Southerners. These fictions followed me into early adulthood when I moved to the South to attend college and teach. I drew on my childhood stereotypes of Southerners to rationalize my new social and racial position as a Black queer living in the South. As I started to question my epistemology through Southern-flavored Hip Hop music and culture, I learned to address and debunk my stereotypes of Southerners. Southern-style Hip Hop music challenged my views of Southern rappers as being uneducated. As I grew older and experienced life from various vantage points, I began to listen to OutKast and Goodie Mob. Once I was able to move beyond their accents, I realized that they articulated the pains of growing up poor and Black, and their message resonated with and inspired me as I found myself and the societal ills of my community within their music. Goodie Mob's gospel and soul music, combined with rap's gritty bravado, took me on an emotional rollercoaster of pleasure, pain, and spirituality. OutKast delivered rhythms to its audience that were more than just words spoken over music but art in its vociferous form. I took note and absorbed every word of these rappers, which demystified my perception of "country" rappers. These rappers' words were creative, clever, intelligent, and rooted in the everyday struggles of being Black and marginalized and created spaces to move beyond the contrived representations of Black youth, which I identified with and was searching for as a young adult.

As I tackled my unfounded beliefs regarding Southerners through Southern rap, my experiences as a queer educator and my perceptions of Southern Black churches—some empirical, some word of mouth—complicated my notions of being Black and queer in the South. Epistemologically, I confronted my childhood normative beliefs of Black Southerners as "country," but as a Black, queer, former elementary school teacher who embodies qualities that are usually associated with maleness (Halberstam, 1998), I always felt out of place in classrooms and within some other Black spaces, specifically Black churches and when working with female Black youth. Sadly, like many queer educators and churchgoers, I faced discrimination because of my lesbian identity that was visible within church and school walls. My anxiety as a Black queer educator only heightened when I moved to the South and experienced first-hand the profound impact of the Black Southern church on the Black community, specifically in regards to issues of queerness. My use of the terms *Black community* and *the Black church* is not to suggest that the Black church or the Black community is monolithic in their thinking or actions regarding homosexuality. However, the terms are utilized throughout the book to generalize my experience growing up Black and queer. The terms *homosexuality* and *homosexual* are used throughout the book because they are the terms widely used within Black churches and communities. I am aware that the field of queer theory no longer uses the term "homosexuality"; however, given the social context of this work, I think it is important to represent the language of the research location and its participants.

## Internalized Homophobia

It is important to note that my fear or shame of being queer in the South manifested from years of being fearful or shameful of being queer anywhere. Psychologists and queer theorists label my shame of being an "out" lesbian as internalized homophobia, which is common among the Lesbian, Gay, Bisexual, Transgender, Queer, Questioning, and Intersex (LGBTQQI) community (DiPlacido, 1998; Meyer, 1995; Meyer & Dean, 1998; Herek, 2004). Internalized homophobia is a complex intrapsychic conflict that can lead to the personal rejection of one's own queerness (Meyer & Dean, 1998). There are three ways that internalized homophobia is manifested within lesbianism: self-hatred and shame (Neisen, 1993; Pharr, 1988), fear of discovery (Loewenstein, 1980; Margolies et al., 1987; Padesky, 1988; Pharr, 1988), and religious condemnation of homosexuality (Gramick, 1983; Neisen, 1993; Ross & Rosser, 1996). Sadly, I have undergone all of the above manifestations of internalized homophobia. According to Szymanski and Chung (2001), internalized homophobia restricts lesbians from fully expressing themselves as such due to the negative assumptions they have acquired regarding queerness while living and learning in heteronormative spaces.

As this chapter progresses, it becomes evident that my discomfort, fear, and shame about researching in the South and working with young girls stemmed from harbored internalized homophobia and my battle with my identity as an African American lesbian within the Black community (i.e., churches, urban schools, and community centers). In addition, as an African American woman, I cannot discuss internalized homophobia without noting the intersecting challenges between these two identities. Black lesbians simultaneously face homophobia and issues of racism, classism, and sexism within our society. Greene (2000) refers to this matrix of oppression as the "triple jeopardy" experience of Black lesbians in that they must integrate and maintain multiple identities. For example, when I enter a room my race, queerness, and sex are visible, and all of these subordinate social constructs are simultaneously functioning for or against me—in my experience, it is more often the latter. Greene adds that

> African American lesbians provide an example of women who face the challenge of integrating more than one salient identity in an environment that devalues them on all levels. . . . The assumption that a lesbian sexual orientation is inconsistent with an authentic "Black" identity represents another expression of homophobia, one that complicates the process of integrating one's sexual orientation identity with other aspects of one's person. Most African American women develop a sense of awareness as an African American person long before they are aware that they are lesbian. This means that the development of healthy coping mechanisms against homophobia may be delayed. (pp. 101–102)

Before beginning my dissertation research, some of my greatest personal struggles involved issues of racial identity. As an African American, race identity is salient (Cross, 1991). It is not only the lens I utilize to understand society, but also one of the first frameworks I learned as a tool to conceptualize my surroundings growing up in a predominantly Black working class neighborhood. Thus, in my life, race trumped queerness. However, as a young adult my experiences as an elementary school teacher and occasional churchgoer—two extremely heteronormative spaces—forced me to address my notions of self.

For years, my lesbian identity took a backseat to my racial identity. Moreover, I put parameters around my lesbian identity, which at times created inner turmoil. For example, I considered myself an "out" lesbian, but only in spaces where I felt comfortable revealing my sexuality. I was not "out" as a teacher, basketball coach, or churchgoer. Although I questioned the extent of my openness, I nonetheless accepted this contradiction. In some respects, I attempted to hide in plain sight. My social context was the barometer of my queerness; my lesbian identity was at times fluid or fixed depending on the environment, individual attitudes, and societal and educational status. For instance, I always felt comfortable discussing my sexuality as a college professor, yet I am still extremely cautious in an elementary or high school classroom with students or colleagues. My guarded sexual identity is grounded in the historical discrimination and oppression LGBTQQI teachers faced due to society's labeling of their sexuality as immoral or sick (Graves, 2009).

## When Literature Is Not Empowering. . . . Can I Get an Amen?

In *The Last Closet: The Real Lives of Lesbian and Gay Teachers* (1996), Rita Kissen argues that queer teachers face the last acceptable form of prejudice in America. Similar works (Jennings, 1994; Harbeck, 1997; Sears, 2002) have documented the challenges of lesbian, gay, bisexual, and transgender or queer educators, as schools represent heteronormative institutions and spaces (Quinn & Meiners, 2009; Rodriguez & Pinar, 2007) where gay students and teachers are pushed to the margins of the classroom. Schools are expected to operate as heterosexual spaces that promote heterosexual values (Khayatt, 1992). Too often, educators who disrupt heteronormativity inside and outside school walls teach in fear (Quinn & Meiners, 2009; Russell, 2008). Queer educators also negotiate the hateful, shameful, and unsubstantiated societal stigma that queerness equates with child sexual abuse (Herek, 1997), which leads many educators, including myself, to be fearful of how parents and school officials perceive the genuine love and care they feel for students. As a result of that apprehension, Duggan (2003) argues that the shame, fear, and loneliness that queer educators encounter push them toward the "new homonormativity," which perpetuates "politics that does not contest dominant heteronormative assumptions and institutions but upholds and sustains them" (p. 50). Thus, heteronormativity is not only sustained within schools but also serves as an unspoken construct by which to measure teachers. For instance, during my teaching student practicum I was politely asked by the school's female principal to "tone" down my masculine dress. The principal informed me that the school's female teachers wore dresses and skirts to work. I did not, so my professionalism was in question. In actuality, what was in question was how my performance of masculinity disrupted the school's heteronormative culture.

Unfortunately, this instance is only one of many experiences that left me constantly troubled in my position as a queer educator and led me to question my visible queerness, which disrupted the school's culture of heteronormativity. When my dress was called into question, so was my sexual identity, which for years I had fought to reserve for intimate settings. This circumstance also triggered my "coming out process" within the workplace, which is tentative and unfinished to this day. As a result, I learned to "actively cope" (Bowleg, Craig, & Burkholder, 2004; Tyler, 1978) within a heterosexual space in order to be professionally successful. Actively coping is defined as a method of minimizing tension or negotiating vicissitudes within one's milieu while also utilizing "internal factors (i.e., self-esteem, race identification, and lesbian identification) and external factors (i.e., social support and perceived availability of LGBT resources) as predictors" (Bowleg, Craig, & Burkholder, 2004, p. 236). Bowleg, Craig, and Burkholder (2004) argue that, due to their multiple oppressed identities, Black lesbians survive heterosexism by actively coping. My active coping strategies comprised avoiding conversations that discussed issues of sexuality, relationships, or marriage around individuals who I thought did not share my views on sexuality. I also did not introduce or publicly recognize my partner as my lover for fear of being labeled as queer.

I found active coping to be useful at church as a way to reduce the tension of anti-homosexual rhetoric. The anti-homosexual rhetoric and sexual politics of the Black church, particularly the theology of Southern Black churches, also influenced (and does so to this day) my constant grappling with my sexuality and my decision to be (or not be) openly gay as a Black woman. Historically, the church represents the oldest and most influential institution in the Black community (Lincoln & Mamiya, 1990). Research shows that church affiliation is vital among Black folks, regardless of socioeconomic levels (Ward, 2005). Thus, the Black church plays a vital role in how Black people conceptualize issues of queerness and homophobia; it has also been instrumental in disseminating the construction of Black masculinity, femininity, and homonormativity (Crawford, Allison, Zamboni, & Soto, 2002; Dyson, 1996; Ward, 2005). What is most remarkable about the Black church as an institution is its reach beyond the church doors. Ward argues:

> But what is also striking is the influence it wields indirectly in the lives of those that are not churchgoers. Even if as adults they no longer embrace the church or religious principles, many blacks have been profoundly influenced by the church ideology and imagery with which they were raised, and this continues to influence their later beliefs and practices. (p. 494)

Even though my family only attended church for funerals and major Christian holidays (Easter and Christmas), my upbringing was grounded in the tenets of Christianity stereotypical of the Black community. Thus, homophobia pervaded my community in upstate New York. As a child, I can remember overhearing numerous adult conversations rooted in biblical scripture that were interpreted as condemnations of homosexuality, which always culminated in the endorsement of homophobia. As a young person struggling to understand my sexuality, I recalled those conversations while I wrestled with my decision to reveal my sexual orientation to my friends and family. When I eventually came out, my friends and family predictably used the Bible to condemn my queerness. My feelings of uneasiness associated with the Black church only grew when I moved to the heart of the South: Atlanta, Georgia. Atlanta is unique in regards to religion and homosexuality because both are unapologetically on display. While it is geographically positioned within the U.S. Bible Belt (made up of socially conservative evangelical Southern states), Atlanta also has the third-largest percentage of gay, lesbian, and bisexual residents among large U.S. cities, as queer folk compose 12.8 percent of the city's population (Williams Institute, 2010). Thus, I was wary of what I might find in this purportedly gay-friendly city that is also home to influential Southern Black church leaders, who utilize their pulpit to preach a message of homophobia and hate.

According to Sears, the South is the bedrock of the Baptist denomination. Southern Baptists are known for their conservative views on sexuality, gender, and sexual practices (Sears, 1991). E. Patrick Johnson (2008), an openly gay Black Southern academic, discusses in his work how it is more difficult to be queer in the South than anywhere else in the United States. He adds that Southern Black ministers, such as Bishop Eddie Long and Rev. Bernice King, eldest daughter of Dr. Martin Luther King, Jr., promote anti-gay sentiments comparable to the Ku Klux Klan's, as both ministers led a 2004 march in Atlanta to protest gay marriage. In 2007, the Southern Poverty Law Center's magazine called Long one of the "most virulently homophobic black leaders in the religiously based anti-gay movement" (R. Robinson, 2010). Long's homophobia came full circle in 2010 when he was accused of coercing young male members of his church into sexual acts. The allegations set off a firestorm within the Black community due to the role of Long's church in the anti-gay Black megachurch movement in the United States.

According to *Ebony* magazine (2004), most Black megachurches have between 10,000 and 30,000 members, and there are over 100 Black megachurches in the United States. Atlanta has two of the largest megachurch congregations—New Birth, Eddie Long's church, and Creflo Dollar's church, World Changers. To date, these churches calculate combined seating to total roughly 30,000 worshippers every Sunday, which does not account for their television membership. Rashad Robinson, Senior Director of Media Programs for the Gay and Lesbian Alliance Against Defamation and *Huffington Post* contributor, stated that Long has told his members,

> "I don't care what scientists say. You can be converted. You were not born that way."
> "Homosexuality and lesbianism are spiritual abortions."
> "God says you deserve death!"

Robinson also added, "By telling families that 'homosexuality is a manifestation of the fallen man,' Bishop Long is implying that they have no choice but to reject their children who identify as LGBT" (2010). In an attempt at full disclosure, I occasionally attended Long's church on the invitation of a close friend prior to my research with the girls. Thus, I can confirm that Long made hateful comments regarding homosexuality and homosexuals; sadly, much of my childhood and adult experiences attending Black churches also used Long's approach. Admittedly, at the time I did not think much of the homophobic condemnation because vile words regarding LGBTQQI people were an unfortunate constant in my church experience.

Needless to say, perhaps, I have found being queer, Black, and spiritual a contradictory space in my struggle to find peace as a lesbian seeking spirituality. My church experience at times created an inner turmoil, since my identity construction rested on my sociocultural context. Long's diatribes against queerness had a profound effect on me; I went to his church in search of love and instead found only hate. His words were one of the major reasons I feared working with young Atlanta teens. Before the allegations against Long his dominance in Atlanta surpassed the pulpit. He was considered a local celebrity, with daily radio programming spots and appearances throughout Atlanta. However, Long's anti-homosexual rhetoric, deeply rooted in theologically-driven homophobia, has been taken to task in light of the charges of sexual misconduct. Political pundit Roland Martin called for Long to step down as church pastor. Moreover, because of Long's highly publicized case, cultural critic and *Washington Post* reporter Eugene Robinson has called for the Black church to rethink its position on homosexuality and same-sex marriage. Increased understanding and acceptance within the Black church of LGBTQQI folks are occurring in small pockets throughout the United States, perhaps even more so now due to Long's scandal. Despite such gradual changes, the church's impact followed me into my research.

As an adult pursuing a doctoral degree that emphasized qualitative research, I thought I had emotionally and psychologically dealt with the stereotypes I had held in the past. However, Lara, Nicole, Lisa, Star, Maxine, and Dee pushed me to examine myself and my worldview beyond the boundaries of an educational researcher and investigate how my perceptions of Southerners limited my research and my initial relationship with the girls.

## Unforeseen Dangers: Ask and Don't Tell

When I started my dissertation research I was both eager and nervous to enter the field. I had known the girls for two years before researching their perceptions regarding Hip Hop and issues of sexuality, race, and gender. However, I had never spoken with them candidly about their thoughts pertaining to Hip Hop, body, and dating. A great deal of my uneasiness was a result of one of my first interactions with Lara, Nicole, Lisa, and Dee. One day during recess, Lara turned to me and asked, "Coach T, you gay?" I paused. I pride myself on being quick-witted, but I was tongue-tied and shocked by the question. I knew that they knew but never thought I would have the question thrown my way or have to verbalize my sexuality. Lara continued, "Why do you have that ring on your finger; who you married to?" I looked down at my hand as if I had forgotten I was wearing a wedding band on my left ring finger. Lara had a small audience; Nicole, Lisa, and Dee waited for my reply. In most circles, I am an open lesbian who is proud of her queerness. However, when children and young adults ask questions pertaining to my sexuality, I tend to freeze up, because thoughts about being perceived as a sexual predator enter my mind. In this instance, I also feared that the girls were homophobic due to their Southern religious views. Instead of answering honestly, I uttered the first thing that rolled off my tongue and hid behind my position as an adult, "I am grown, and y'all are in my business." By not answering the questions, I answered the questions. The girls walked away laughing as if they knew all along. They just wanted to hear it from my own mouth. I felt like someone in an ABC afterschool special about how not to approach gay and lesbian students in high school. This exchange between me and the girls happened within the first month of my working at the center, and it continued to shape how I interacted with the girls. From that point on, I walked on eggshells around them. My field memos illustrate my trepidation of the girls once I started my research.

> Why do I feel the need to change my dress around the girls? Like that will change who I am. They know I know they know I am a lesbian, so what am I afraid of? (10/07)

> Dr. E is pushing me to interview the girls more. I have to make an effort. I know girls have a lot to say that would be beneficial to my work, but I am afraid of the personal questions that will be directed at me. (1/08)

> I have to make the connection I have with the boys with the girls. (1/08)

My dissertation advisor, Dr. E, pushed me to connect with the girls at the center. I was apprehensive for many reasons but mostly because of the nature of my interview questions. Asking straight Black girls about how they view their bodies in relation to the hypersexual space of Hip Hop made me uncomfortable. I was worried that the girls would misconstrue my line of questioning because I was a queer woman. There was also a cultural disconnect when the girls learned I was from upstate New York. To them, all New Yorkers were overconfident. I too was guilty of such perceptions. Although my definition of "country" had evolved because of rap, I relied on the label to make it easier for me to overlook the girls and justify my avoidance of the issue. This "easy way out" changed when Lara asked me why I did not interview the girls the way I interviewed the boys. In that moment, I felt ashamed. I was silencing a group of young girls because of my own insecurities of being openly queer and working with the same sex. As a result, Lara, Nicole, Lisa, Dee, Maxine, and Star took it upon themselves to form an informal and covert Gay-Straight Alliance.

## Safe Spaces

After Lara's comment, I started interviewing the girls on a regular basis—still cautious, but pushing myself beyond my fear. My memos speak to my struggle in opening up to the girls.

> Today Lisa and Maxine had a lot to say about everything. They challenged me to ask questions beyond the surface about sex, relationships, and their body. I can't turn back now. (11/07)

> I wish the boys spoke as much as the girls. The relationship I have with the boys centers around sports. The girls want to tell me everything. I should have interviewed them a long time ago. I am floored by the girls' candidness on the subject matter. (1/08)

> I am starting to see that the girls could care less about my sexual orientation; they have a story they want to tell and I am the only one listening. (1/08)

A closer examination of my field notes reveals my habitual gravitation to place the boys at the forefront of my research in order to make me, the researcher, feel more at ease. As a result, I left the young girls within the study feeling alienated due to my unwillingness to tackle my contentious positionality toward Southern females, whom I presumed would reject me. Looking back, I was drawn to the boys because of our superficial connection to sports, which was a major part of my identity. In actuality, I used that connection to hide the fact that I was fearful of the girls' perception of me. As I began to interview the girls more, I learned they cared less about me and their surrounding community's homophobia and more about telling their story. As a result of the girls' yearning to be heard, a funny thing began to occur: They had conversations surrounding issues of homosexuality with me in the room but never engaged me in the conversations. For example, Lisa told Dee about two girls at their school who were openly gay. Lisa told Dee that she did not care that the girls were gay, and Dee agreed. Lisa and Lara, while in my earshot, had a discussion about two girls who were holding hands in the hallways at their school. This particular exchange between the girls happened twice while I was interacting with the students. Both girls stated that they did not care about the girls' sexual orientation and that people should have the right to do whatever they pleased. By having informal conversations that placed me in the background, the girls were able to express to me their feelings about homosexuality, which were rooted in social justice, fairness, human rights, and solidarity. The girls not only demonstrated a belief that the individuals within the LGBTQQI community should have the right to love whomever they chose but also thought it was unfair that rights were denied to LGBTQQI community members.

Throughout the study, my relationship with the girls evolved as they challenged me to view them beyond my twenty-six years of prejudice toward Southerners. Ironically, I was learning for the first time how to position my sexual identity, by way of six Southern heterosexual girls. Through their conversations, HCC—which was a heteronormative space—became a safe space for me as a queer researcher. Through indirect yet deliberate dialogue, the teens informed me that I was accepted as a lesbian within their community. As the girls thoughtfully and openly challenged homophobia, I was the one who refused to interrupt heteronormativity because of my internalized homophobia and fear that my sexuality might impede the completion of my dissertation; this parallels my student teaching experience referred to earlier. Thus, the moments in which I have been most afraid to challenge or interrupt heteronormativity were moments in which I was being evaluated for terminal degrees—that is, when my endeavors for my future were on the line. As a young professional in the field of education, I felt silenced by my positionality, upbringing, and experiences within Black churches and schools.

Looking back, I tried to conceal or downplay my queerness in an effort to obtain my degree by keeping my professional and sexual identifications separate and protecting them from interrogation. In general, educators should not have to choose between furthering their careers and hiding who they are. Moreover, my refusal to engage these six girls in a dialogue regarding sexual freedom and choice is exactly where I failed them. My fears as a queer educator and my stereotypes of Black Southern life, influenced by my perceptions of the Black church not only limited my research but also my personal growth as a Black woman determined to challenge societal norms. Hearing pastors like Long and King preach anti-homosexual sermons that not only condemned me to Hell but also questioned my very humanity were more than hurtful. Their venomous diatribes made me second-guess myself and my interactions with individuals I thought agreed with them. With these fears in mind, I entered into my dissertation research assuming that the girls echoed Long's sentiments toward homosexuality, whose hateful words haunted my life as I researched in fear.

## Work in Progress

Initially, in retrospect, I not only neglected the girls as a researcher but also, most importantly, as an educator. They explicitly chose language that confronted heteronormativity and supported me in order to address issues of homophobia. Haberman (2000) contends that "language is not an innocent reflection of how we think. The terms we use control our perceptions, shape our understanding, and lead us to particular proposals for improvement" (p. 203). The girls' language was a direct reflection of my unwillingness to interview them more, or with the same consistency that I interviewed the boys. In response, the girls, through their seeking equity, deliberately addressed my internalized homophobia that had kept them from telling me their stories of being young, Black, female, heterosexual, and a part of the Hip Hop culture. I struggled with the tension of being open with the girls regarding my sexuality, even as they created a space that disrupted heteronormativity. My past perceptions, homophobia, and tangled identity, influenced by my current situation, translated into heterosexual hegemony where heterosexuality is not just the norm but also a heavy expectation (Frank, 1987). In other words, I attempted to embody the normative gendered constructs that privileged heteronormativity. I socially resisted confronting these constructs due to years of fear built on whispers of hate. I thought I knew who I was until I met these six young women. The girls, through their words and behavior, allowed me to face my fears and take a hard look at myself, in an effort to understand the place from which my fears derived. Their actions tore down decades of stereotypes and unfounded judgments I had regarding Southerners as well as my own tension surrounding being openly gay in the South. The teens were willing to disrupt fixed notions of sexuality that were pervasive throughout their community and engage in a dialogue in which they created new spaces for the subjects of desire, sexuality, and identity (Sumara & Davis, 1999).

Furthermore, the girls disrupted and challenged the cultural norms of the Black community's perspectives on queerness. Their thoughts illustrate how a growing number of young Black individuals are pulling away from tropes that are divisive and homophobic. It was amazing to interact with youth who not only shared my cultural background (working class, public school education, dysfunctional family) but who also had insightful ideas regarding sexuality that my generation failed to grasp, even though I am not sure it was ever within our reach. Thus Lara, Nicole, Lisa, Dee, Maxine, and Star were engaging in elements of queer theory while I rested in what Halley (1993, p. 83) calls "heterosexual bribes," in which public performance is restricted to proper heterosexual identity. One of my greatest flaws existed in my belief that I could hide as a lesbian in plain sight, only confronting my racial identity and leaving my lesbian identity behind. By hiding, I missed opportunities to re-narrate my closeted performance at HCC and engage in dialogue with fearless, open-minded young women. In retrospect, this learning experience was more my loss than theirs. After the girls created a space for me to research, my relationship with them was much more fluid. They shared with me their thoughts and experiences regarding Hip Hop music and culture as young women negotiating, resisting, and navigating its messages of social inequality, racism, body, sexism, politics, class, and gender.

*Chapter Five*

# Where Are the White Girls?

### Choice, Individualism, and Meritocracy: Let's Play the Blame Game

To set the stage for this chapter and provide a visual example of the type of videos the girls watched, I have chosen a video by the rapper, Plies, one of the more popular videos viewed by the girls in 2007 and 2008. The girls also watched videos by Lil' Wayne, 50 Cent, and Soulja Boy; however, many of the girls, especially Dee, Lisa, Nicole, and Lara, thought Plies was attractive and referenced his songs and persona frequently. One of Plies's popular songs during the time of the study was "Shawty." In the song, Plies, a Black rapper, graphically details having sex with Black women, who earn the so-called affectionate title of Shawty. In the video, Plies rescues a Black woman who is penniless. In so doing, he hands her a bankroll of money and a car as a quid pro quo for sex. There are no White women in the video, and one of the Black women in it has a low-paying job as a dishwasher. Plies rescues her by giving her money and making her one of his many girlfriends or Shawties. Plies is the handsome prince who saves beautiful, curvy Black women from poverty or low-paying jobs. The video implies that without Plies's money, which is tied to sex work, these Black women would never escape poverty. Unfortunately, many rap videos subscribe to a similar formula. When Star was asked what she thought about Black women who were featured in rap videos like "Shawty," she said, "Being [a] Black [woman] is being wild, actin' a fool" (Interview, 2007). Star added that the Black women in the videos "need to put some clothes on" (Interview, 2007). When I asked Dee about the women in music videos, she added, "You don't see no White women taking up their shirts; it's usually on those videos you see Black women" (Interview, 2007). At this point in the interview, I did not ask Dee about race. She instantly began answering my questions through the lens of race. When I followed up with the question, "Why don't you see White women?" Dee added, "They got better thangs to do"

(Interview, 2007). When I asked her what "Black women had to do," she said, "actin' a fool and not going to school" (Interview, 2007). Utilizing the lyrics and imagery of Plies and countless other rap videos, Dee and Star blamed the individual women for their choices without factoring in the complex systems of poor schools, patriarchy, and the male-dominated industry of rap.

Another influence on the teens' perceptions was the lack of exposure to Black women who counter the images of oversexed and unintelligent women, even though these girls lived in a metropolis with an overwhelming number of successful, highly educated Black women. The absence of diverse representations of Black women in rap videos, along with countless billboards in Atlanta that show women of color as strippers and adult entertainers, led the girls to assume that many women of color freely chose this line of work and could have "easily" entered into a career as a lawyer or a doctor. Dee expressed her view of choice by noting, "You [Black women in videos] could have been in school being a lawyer or something and still making money enjoying your life. Instead you're doing it another way" (Interview, 2008). Dee did not take into account poor schooling, gender, class, and racial power structures that can prevent women of color from becoming lawyers. Thus, the ideas of choice, merit, and individualism permeated the teens' perceptions of the women in rap videos like "Shawty." Choice, individualism, and meritocracy are all major components of America's lexicon because they are fundamental to the neo-conservative "bootstraps model" of achievement, which was established by the dominant hegemonic groups in order to control the marginalized masses (Omi & Winant, 1994). The bootstraps model is grounded in the belief that marginalized groups are willing to accept the norms and values of the dominant culture and press on to succeed despite systematic oppression (Omi & Winant, 1994). As a result, low-quality education, dilapidated communities, poor health care, and violence become normalized as "general circumstances" that marginalized groups must endure and overcome (Omi & Winant, 1994). In the eyes of the neo-conservative framework, these "common circumstances" are a result of poor choices made by persons in a marginalized group such as African Americans (Omi & Winant, 1994).

Furthermore, Hip Hop itself is grounded in the conservative principles of individualism, meritocracy, and capitalism, along with American values of sexism, misogyny, patriarchy, classism, materialism, and racism. Thus, the provocative sound and imagery of Hip Hop are as American as apple pie or baseball. However, equally, Hip Hop aligns with democratic socialist politics that highlight the need for a redistribution of wealth, resources, and power. Hip Hop also speaks to the concerns of the poor, unemployed, and disenfranchised. This competing duality of Left and Right politics is why Hip Hop is so infectious to urban youth, who then struggle to unpack Hip Hop's messages of success, wealth, and womanhood laced with American values and Black faces. Dee's comments are grounded in an Americanism that is deeply planted within the rap industry and society at large. This observation is not to over-generalize Dee's conceptual framework in regards to gender oppression; rather, it shows how, within the context of rap alongside her neo-conservative perspectives, she unequally contrasted two career paths that are often chosen or not chosen because of education and class or lack thereof. In Dee's opinion, the women who appeared in rap videos actually chose to participate in their own exploitation instead of pursuing more lucrative professions. Dee's idea of choice did not allow her to address the fact that, while women may have the option of choice, the possibilities are limited. hooks (1994) argues that

> [m]any women in this society do have choices (as inadequate as they are), therefore exploitation and discrimination are words that more accurately describe the lot of women collectively in the United States. . . . Under capitalism, patriarchy is structured so that sexism restricts women's behavior in some realms even as freedom from limitations is allowed in other spheres. (p. 5)

No matter if it is in Atlanta or elsewhere, women face undeniable inequalities and limited choices within the universal systems of capitalism and patriarchy. The larger issue at play within Dee's comments, and the comments that follow by Nicole and Lara, is the blame game. Women routinely blame other women for poor decisions without contextualizing society. Women place blame utilizing insulated, complex systems of oppression. As women blame other women for personal and societal shortcomings, social constructs continue to remain unexamined and undiscussed. Thus, women use frameworks such as meritocracy to justify individual failures rather than look to systemic forms of oppression.

In another interview, Nicole and Lara further explained youth's beliefs surrounding choice, merit, and the cycle of blame.

> We're being disrespectful to ourselves and to other people. We be looking like freaks, and giving it away for money. (Nicole, Interview, 2008)

> We have common sense but we just don't use it at the time. We make wrong . . . we make wrong choices like we don't think before we do. We don't then think about the consequences. (Lara, Interview, 2008)

These quotes demonstrate the girls' common view that the Black women who perform in rap videos have made "wrong choices" because of a lack of money or poor decision-making skills. They also stress that Black women do not understand the consequences of their actions. In addition, these comments also speak to how the girls use morality to judge women who danced in videos and appeared in rap videos. When Nicole says that women "are giving it away for money," she is implying that the Black women who appear in videos are having sex freely without having any type of committed relationship with male rappers. Nicole's line of thought is an example of the neo-conservative ideology that is built on the tenets of social conservatism, which places heavy emphasis on waiting until marriage to have sex and the elimination of pornography and promiscuity. These frameworks promote "traditional Southern values," which the culture of rap and the city of Atlanta contradict directly as a subversive space within America's Bible Belt. Simply put, the girls in the study judged the women in rap videos who danced partially naked as being morally corrupt because of their own Southern Christian views, which are rooted in mainstream African American values. Growing up in a city where the selling of adult entertainment is part of the city's ethos, the girls assumed that a great number of Black women lack financially stable livelihoods, which is one of the themes generated by the Plies video. Lara stated, "Yeah, 'cause they know like blacks, African Americans will be the first . . . trying to make money" (Interview, 2007). At no time during the interviews did the youth differentiate among Black women; they categorized all Black women as individuals who make poor decisions. The teens' neo-conservative worldviews informed their critiques of the Black women who appeared in rap videos. They did not once consider the corporate manufacturing of rap or the notion that culture-industry laborers created the narrative of rap and, therefore, only cast scantily-clad Black women in order to sell their physical appearance as a racial commodity that, in turn, maintains the male gaze (Fitts, 2008). Melyssa Ford, one of rap's premier video vixens, told *King* magazine in 2005 that

> I have seen a couple that definitely fit the stereotype of being a video ho. But the majority of the video girls that I've been around are very smart, self-respecting individuals who often are college-educated. And that is the truth. The whole video ho thing is such bullshit. (quoted in Story, 2007)

Despite Ford's assertions, culture-industry laborers of rap sell a fantasy for male viewing pleasure, and the image of self-sufficient, educated, fully dressed Black women does not fit the bill. As the girls examined rap, neo-conservative ideas of self-responsibility, colorblindness, and traditional individualism (Omi & Winant, 1994) influenced their rationalizations of Black women's involvement in what they considered a demeaning career. These ideological formations preserve the neo-conservative agenda, while Black youth serve as scapegoats to explain America's social ills. Giroux (2006) argues that neo-conservative thinking "ignores how political and economic institutions with their circuits of repression and disposability and their technologies of punishment, connect and condemn the fate of many impoverished youth of color" (p. 3). The framework that the teens employed to demonize women in rap videos dismisses the role of dominant institutions and the permanent fixture of racism that denies the social and economic progress of Blacks (Bell, 1992). The teens are unaware of rap music as a space overwhelmed with contrived representations that are "subject to market concerns of white supremacist, patriarchal, multinational, [and] corporate capitalism" (Miller-Young, 2008, p. 263). To simply state that video girls made the choice to be objectified oversimplifies the mistreatment of women—past and present. The teens believed that Black women chose to be in rap videos because of their various shortcomings, a notion informed by neo-conservative thought. This assumption also influenced their beliefs about Black and White women. Although rap videos are what the girls "choose" to consume, I would argue that they did not have much of a choice. Television programs that are geared toward their age group and racial demographic are saturated with materialism, sex, drugs, violence, and Black women as sexual objects. The girls are not left with many choices as to what to watch as young African American girls looking to Black popular culture for insight about race, gender, class, and sexuality.

## The Power of Not Seeing

The girls' limited exposure to White women in rap videos, coupled with the gentrification that was taking place in their community and their social conservative values created a worldview that White women make better choices and are too financially secure to partake in the exploitative industry of rap. Not seeing White women in rap videos, but in their neighborhood driving expensive cars and living in upscale homes, created a good girl–bad girl duality, with race as the marker of distinction.

> Because they're [White women] more intelligent. They [White women] think before they talk. . . . They get their education. (Lara, Interview, 2008)

> And they [White women] don't need money like we do. . . . I think that the White people, they keep their body as a temple because they don't show their body off and all that. (Maxine, Interview, 2008)

> They [White women] don't show cleavage—only cleavage they show, the cleavage they show is little bitty skirts but other than that, little shirts and stuff they won't. (Star, Interview, 2008)

The study's findings echo the 1997 findings of Gan, Zillman, and Mitrook, who found that White youth who watched sexually enticing rap videos depicting Black women as oversexed and promiscuous subsequently saw Black women as "distinctly unfavorable" (p. 381). In particular, they found that White youth generalized all Black women as having negative traits in the area of sexual immorality. Stephens and Phillips (2005) argue that "beliefs and attitudes about the sexuality of African American women appear to be sanctioned by a culture that continues to embrace stereotypes about race and sexuality" (p. 5). This trend is made especially clear when one scans the content of rap videos. Another popular video that served as a site of race and gender education for the girls was Soulja Boy's "Crank That," which depicts Black girls dressed as dancers for the rapper. Stephens and Phillips (2005) contend that "[t]he good, innocent, virgin continues to be an idealized image of womanhood associated with White females, but unattainable for African American females" (p. 4). The researchers add, "Differentiating African American adolescent women's sexuality from White women's reinforces their positions as individuals standing on the margins of society, clarifying its boundaries" (p. 4).

The teens' remarks above coupled with the rap videos discussed provide evidence of Stephens and Phillips's claim, as well as Gan, Zillman, and Mitrook's (1997) proposition that youth who engage with images of Black women as male sexual accessories view Black women as inferior to their White counterparts. Their examination led to the good girl–bad girl duality: These youth believed that White women escaped dressing promiscuously in movies and rap videos because White women are inherently more moral and are better decision makers than Black women. Like many of us, the teens viewed television through a racial lens; therefore, they watched programs geared toward their race and age. Television shows or movies that depicted White women in sexual, provocative ways were not a part of the teens' media diet, which led them to believe that

White women did not take part in overly sexualized behavior. These racist and unempirical assumptions are an aspect of neo-conservatism that denies Black women the opportunity to debunk the recycled stereotype of promiscuity. This internalizing process, coupled with negative essentialist ideas of Blackness, can lower the self-esteem of young Black girls as they use rap to compare and contrast race and gender norms (hooks, 1992). What follows is an excerpt from an interview with Maxine in which she implicitly illustrated the either/or dichotomy that led to her essentialist ideas of White and Black women in terms of education, economics, and social status. I quote this interview at length because it embodies Maxine's thought process and how she came to understand White and Black intellectual positions through rap videos.

> Tina: I was looking back when I interviewed you before and you said something that I've got to ask some questions about. You said something that White women are smart because they don't show their bodies the way Black women do on T.V. Do you remember you said that?
>
> Maxine: Oh yeah.
>
> Tina: Why did you say that?
>
> Maxine: Because like it's all about money and most of African American girls drop out of school and stuff and make the wrong choices. And it's all a part of life but you don't see the White women dropping out of school. They go all the way through and make straight A's and do what their parents want them to do.
>
> Tina: When you say "we're" being—who?
>
> Maxine: Women, us women (*pointing back and forth*).
>
> Tina: Us women, Black women?
>
> Maxine: Yes, us as Black women are kind of like, we're—how can I say this—we're giving people a sign how we want to be treated, how we represent ourselves basically.
>
> Tina: How do you think we represent ourselves?
>
> Maxine: Well, it depends on how you wear your clothes. So if you wear like some girls in the videos and stuff they wear like tube tops and stuff and then like real short shorts and then regular women wear long pants, not really tight.
>
> Tina: What do you mean regular women?

Maxine: Kind of like basically White kids or sometimes Black; it depends on half and half. So it's like, I don't know, it's basically like you see more Black people wearing that than White.

Tina: You see more Black people wearing?

Maxine: Tube tops and stuff on videos and stuff. You never see White girls on there.

Tina: Why do you think you don't see White girls doing that?

Maxine: Because they're smart and intelligent not to do that. They go through school and do what their parents ask and be what they want to be so that they can be able to get where they want to be, not by doing pop, lock [dancing] and drop it [dancing] and stuff, making money.

Tina: So you think White girls are able to know the difference?

Maxine: Because they think before they do. What they do, it's like a plan, a life plan that they do that they have before they—they think before they do basically and they figure it out with their parents and themselves, and basically they go to good schools, get their education, be what they want to be, then think about what they can do other than being out there.

Tina: Okay, three White girls just walked by. What do you think about them?

Maxine: Intelligent, radiant, smart, um, very smart, because they go to a private school and you have to take tests to go in a private school, and the tests are very hard. I can say that from my understanding. And basically they're mindful and they listen, then always talk.

Tina: Do you think you're smart like those three girls that just walked by?

Maxine: Yes. I know I'm smart. I'm really smart.

Tina: So you know that?

Maxine: Yes.

Tina: Why do you think so highly of them [White girls]?

Maxine: I don't know, they [White girls] just are.

- (Interview, 2008)

Before we analyze the conversation above, I think it is important to share my field memo I wrote after my conversation with Maxine.

> Today was tough. Maxine sat across from me today and described a world where Black women are inferior to White women. What I found most compelling was her candor. She was confident in her assumptions regarding women of color and blames them solely. At one point in the interview she pointed to me, informing me that women in videos give "us" all a bad name. Maxine is one of the brightest girls at the center, but feels less bright because of her race, the race of the tutors, and the images in rap that reinforce her thinking of inferiority. . . . We are failing Maxine, myself included.
> (Field memo, 2008)

There is a lot to unpack within this conversation between Maxine and me, but first, my field notes provide some important context. The three White girls who walked by us were tutors. The tutors at the center were all White, and most of them were young girls between the ages of fifteen and eighteen years old. Most of them drove expensive cars, attended private schools, wore pristine uniforms, and were college bound. Thus, the race and class of the tutors created a racially inferior setting for the Black girls who attended the center. They, on the other hand, rode the bus to the center, viewed college as unobtainable, and were tutored by White girls of the same age. Due to the tutor population, Maxine and other girls endured a constant reminder of their inferiority. Additionally, by not seeing White women in rap videos or inferior positions on a daily basis, Maxine presumed that they were more educated and possessed the ability to make choices irrespective of life circumstances, which played out at the center. The interview also speaks to Maxine's criterion of who can be a role model. I was sitting right across from Maxine, a former college basketball player and college graduate who was pursuing her Ph.D., but I was not a viable candidate for role model because I was not financially successful. The tutors' race and class, my sexuality, the city of Atlanta that sells sex in the colors of Brown and Black, the lack of community role models, and rap music's demeaning portrayal of women of color created the "perfect" storm for the girls' feelings of inadequacy.

Moreover, Maxine's statement, "And it's all a part of life but you don't see the White women dropping out of school," speaks volumes to the embedded neo-conservative ideas she possessed. "It's all part of life" legitimates the systemic social ills of Blacks and also demonstrates that she subscribes to the "bootstraps model" of overcoming all obstacles in order to excel. This statement also emphasizes the dichotomous nature of Maxine's belief system: Although she feels Black women have a harder life than White women, she still holds Black women to the same standards as their White counterparts. Maxine's words also illustrate how she experiences the race distinction, in that she views White women as superior to Black women because of their dress, education, and financial stability.

In addition, the youth perceived White women's absence from rap videos as empowering and indicative of their better decision-making skills when compared to Black women. Maxine thought it was a White girl's choice not to appear in the rap videos. Lisa further explained the youth's essentialist notions of Black and White in popular culture.

> Like okay, take like the movies. They might have, like, the White students, they might have on, like, blue jeans and long shirts but, like, the Black people in a movie, they might have on little shorts and they play like the freak in the movie or something like that. Like they have on the little halter tops and shorts. (Interview, 2008)

The movies that Lisa watched informed her ideas of Black and White womanhood. As a frame of reference, Lisa drew on movies and rap videos to compare and judge Black and White women by the clothes that Black women wear or do not wear, which led to the girls making observations regarding Black women's morals, cultural capital, and sexual lives. A person's cultural capital is linked to their "ways of talking, acting, and socializing, as well as language practices, values, and styles of dress and behavior" (McLaren, 1994, p. 198). As a result of the women's dress in rap videos, the teens perceived their cultural capital as inadequate. Lisa experienced movies that portrayed Black women as "freaks" and White women as wearing less revealing clothes, which she believed gave them elevated cultural capital. Nicole stated, "[White women] not goin' be like that. [White women] might have on a suit or something, like, dressy" (Interview, 2008). Nicole's experiences with White women led her to believe that White women dress in a sophisticated and smart manner. She concluded that White women make conscious decisions to dress like professionals, while Black women choose to dress promiscuously. The manner in which women dress in rap videos and movies also informed the teens about the values of Black and White women and caused them to form distinctions regarding substantial traits based on superficial presentation.

Outside of choice, these six young women did not recognize the countless other reasons why White women do not appear in rap videos. The racially calculated space of rap is flooded with culture-industry laborers who sell not only music but also a disguised extension of continued male dominance and racism (Fitts, 2008). As Collins (2004) argues,

> [t]he new racism also relies more heavily on mass media to reproduce and disseminate the ideologies needed to justify racism. . . . A generation of young African American men and women who were born after the struggles for civil rights, Black power, and African nation-state independence has come of age under this new racism. Referred to as the hip-hop generation, this group has encountered, reproduced, and resisted new forms of racism that continue to rely on ideas about Black sexuality. Expecting a democratic, fair society with equal economic opportunities, instead, this group faced disappearing jobs, crumbling schools, drugs, crime, and the weakening of African American institutions. (pp. 34–35)

The youth in this study understood mass media to be fair, with equal chances of mobility for all; racism was not a part of their conceptual equation. They also neglected to account for rap as a corporate-manipulated space filled with repackaged contemporary images of racism and sexism (Collins, 2004; West, 2001).

The teens in the study are intelligent young women who utilized frameworks learned from their teachers, parents, and society in order to deconstruct Black and White women. Their unawareness of the systems of racism and sexism within Hop Hip falls on us, myself included, as educators, who were also educated without critical examinations of the media. Therefore, the primary reason students are unaware of the inequalities that exist in our racially charged media is because of us—adults in a position to engage students in conversations and class discussions who are unaware of the power of critical media literacy. As the study reveals, these six young women were unacquainted with gender oppression and the new forms of racism perpetuated by rap's depiction of Black sexuality infused with neo-conservative thinking. These findings demonstrate that school leaders must begin to understand that they can no longer ignore rap music. The oral and visual messages youth experience through rap artists and Black popular culture have an impact on their ideas of self, Black womanhood, racial perceptions, and society. Next, I explore how rap videos' images impact the girls' perceptions of the Black female body, standards of beauty, desirability, and dating.

AN
ADULT
ENTERTAINMENT
VIP
EXCLUSIVE

## *Chapter Six*

# Body Image, Relationships, Desirability, and Ass

### Baby, I Was Born This Way (Maybe): Junk in the Trunk or the Lack Thereof

In conjunction with rap videos that highlight a Black woman's butt ("Da' Butt," E.U., 1988; "Rump Shaker," Wreckx-n-Effect, 1993; "Big Ole Butt" LL Cool J, 1995; "Daisy Dukes," Duice, 1992; "Baby Got Back," Sir Mix-A-Lot, 1992; "Bootylicious," Destiny's Child, 2001; "Donk," Soulja Boy, 2007; and "Drop It Low," Ester Dean featuring Chris Brown, 2009), the girls live in Atlanta, where they are bombarded with billboards, advertisements, and strip clubs that emphasize the backsides of women of color. These images are not only permanent fixtures in the city but, more important, to the girls these images represent the Black female body as seen by mainstream America, their community, the opposite sex, and the girls themselves. When I began to engage them in discussions surrounding body and what it meant to be Black women, many of the girls' answers centered on the backside of the Black female body, which mimics the rap industry's and the city's obsession with ass. Hip Hop's celebration of curvy women of color is another space, much like at strip clubs, where Hip Hop music and culture depart from the mainstream to create new notions regarding Black female sexuality and desirability. However, while this new frontier disturbs historical notions of Black beauty and body, it reinforces the narrative that all Black women have bodies similar to or just like the women who appear in videos or grace billboards and magazine ads.

This monolithic representation of the Black woman's body created an essentialized view of such to the girls. When asked to explain what it meant to be a Black girl, Lara stated, "You gotta have body to be Black. If you ain't got body, you lame" (Interview, 2007). Nicole added, "Like, you know, if you Black, you got a body, whatever" (Interview, 2007). To these girls having "body," which is a euphemism for a large butt, is a vital component of Black womanhood. In another interview, Lisa's comments explicitly addressed not only the notion of biological essentialism but also the societal pressure to conform to rap's sexual scripts. She stated, "You ain't got no big butt, you ain't no Black person, you know" (Interview, 2008). Maxine stated, "Ya Black girls have butts" (Interview, 2007). Lisa and Maxine internalized the notion that being a Black woman meant added emphasis on the "body," or the butt. The idea that having a large butt is a prerequisite for a Black woman is evident in Lisa's words. In a similar vein, Lisa also spoke of the family stigma attached to a Black female who is not biologically endowed with a "big butt." The following extract from an interview with Lisa illustrates the communal pressure and expectations from other Black women in her family to look the part of a Black woman. In this interview, Lisa spoke about how her female family members chastised her for not having a body that they considered worthy of the family name.

> Like, in my family, most of the women got big hips and big butts. Like my family be like, you ain't no Johnson, be doing stuff like that. And they be saying stuff like, in my family like other people, like in my family like in the country. The Johnsons got the big hips and the big butt. (Interview, 2007)

At times, Lisa questioned fitting into her family as a Black woman because she did not have the required biological characteristics. She later stated in the same interview that "That's just like saying, oh I'm probably going to get some big butt and hips you know, just to fit in" (Interview, 2007). Although the latter comment was made in a jovial manner, it speaks to the social pressures and the pervasive influence of sexual scripting on youth culture. Nicole, Lisa's sister, went further by adding, "Black women have body. That's how we shape" (Interview, 2007). Even when White women appeared in rap videos, the girls interpreted the positioning of White girls behind the Black women to be due to their lack of having the right body type to be at the video's center. To the girls, White women in rap videos are secondary to Black women because White women lack "body."

> Yeah, the White girls are in the back of the video (Nicole, Interview, 2008).
> Probably 'cause they don't have no body, you know, like I ain't sayin' they don't have bodies but you know they're not like Black women. (Lisa, Interview, 2008)

> Like Jezzy videos, stuff like that, you don't see no White girls really. Not really, but it be a few of them but it be really the Black ones out there. (Dee, Interview, 2007).

These words show that rap videos fuel the concept of biological essentialism. To the girls, White women are biologically incapable of having a body like Black women. Even when the girls themselves did not have bodies like the girls in the videos, they still theorized that all Black women have body.

To the girls in the study, Black women must possess large buttocks in order to be considered an authentic Black woman. According to Gaunt (2006), as informed by the work of Bem (1993), biological essentialism "rationalizes and legitimizes gender polarization and male dominance by treating them as the natural and inevitable consequences of the intrinsic biological natures of women and men" (p. 524). Biological essentialism is constructed around peoples' belief systems and culturally embedded gender lenses within our society (Bem, 1993; Gaunt, 2006). For example, Lara stated, "It's all about the body" (Interview, 2007), and Lisa followed by adding, "Yeah, 'cause like they say the Black ones got big butts" (Interview, 2007). When Lisa is speaking of "they," she is not only speaking of Black males. As shown above by Lisa's earlier comments regarding her family's perceptions of body, Black women in her family also have internalized the stereotypes surrounding the Black female body. To these young women, being a Black woman was more than just having Black skin—it was also about body.

### Finding a Mate for the Around the Way Girl

No matter one's age, dating is stressful. For teens, the stress is heightened because of societal pressure to act and look a particular way. For the girls, dating was another space where Hip Hop's manufactured messages about women of color played a role in how they found and pursued a mate. For example, when I asked Dee about finding a boyfriend, she candidly responded, "If you got the biggest booty or whatever, you theirs on the block, yeah they go for like the biggest butt. They like girls with big butts" (Dee, Interview, 2007). In referring to males and their view of desirable female characteristics, Dee illustrated her belief that Black women must possess large buttocks in order for males to see them as attractive. This conception is a consequence of the prevalent images in rap music. During numerous interactions with Dee, she spoke openly about feeling frustrated with males who only showed interest in young women with "body" who mirrored video models. She stated, "Yeah, they don't go for me, they think they going to get a girl that look like a video girl" (Dee, Interview, 2008). Since Dee did not fit the body type of a "video girl," she found herself rejected by males she was interested in dating. When I asked Lisa why she thought males only found females with large backsides attractive, she responded, "Because 'dem songs. Them songs tell them to treat us like that" (Interview, 2008). According to Lisa, rap music is responsible for the body norms to which males subjugate their female counterparts. In short, Lisa blamed rap music for the mistreatment of women. To her, rap songs tell young boys how to relate to women. When I asked Lisa what she meant by "treating us like that," she said, "like we [Black girls] all about sex and stuff." Lara added to Lisa's feelings of being treated like a sex object: "They think we gonna have sex with them because 'dem songs" (Interview, 2008). The girls further explained what boys thought about them because of rap music's representations of women of color.

> Probably that we're [Black women] freaks and we reveal a lot. (Nicole, Interview, 2008)

> People think you gotta dance, you gotta sing, and got a body . . . butt. Then you beautiful. (Lisa, Interview, 2008)

Lisa's words speak volumes to what her world, as well as Black popular culture, sees as beautiful and desirable. Lisa's requirements for beauty were exactly what Black popular culture deems to be acceptable standards of beauty. Lisa could only interpret what is given.

Examples like Beyoncé, Jennifer Lopez, and Rihanna underscore Lisa's point: They are popular as singers but are as equally popular for their appearances and voluptuous body types. Lara and Nicole explained how males whom the girls were interested in dismissed them because they did not resemble the body types the males considered desirable.

> Just like the girls in the video, like they act like they put they selves out there like they look for attention, like and boys see that and they maybe want to talk to them. Like a girl might wear to school a real short skirt and no legging and probably a have a big butt . . . and it draw attention to her and then they try to talk to her. (Nicole, Interview, 2007)

> It's all about the body. . . . They like chasing the bigger girl than a skinny girl. (Lara, Interview, 2007)

Dee and Lisa offered the following:

> All dudes grab on girls butts and be nasty. They don't care. (Dee, Interview, 2008)

> They think they can just touch us. (Lisa, Interview, 2008)

They are describing sexual harassment, which takes place in our schools every day, no matter the racial makeup of the school. Their words are disturbing yet constant with my experience as a teacher and the work of Jody Miller. In *Getting Played: African American Girls, Urban Inequality, and Gendered Violence* (2008), Miller takes an in-depth look at the lives of inner-city Black girls who experience sexual harassment and assault because of their exposure to gender, class, and racial inequalities in their violent neighborhoods. As a former elementary school teacher, I can remember reprimanding boys on a weekly basis for inappropriately touching girls. My school did not have a sexual harassment policy and was more concerned with test scores, so more often than not reports of the mistreatment of girls fell on deaf ears.

The girls struggled to find male mates because their bodies did not meet the requirements of what the rap industry considers a Black woman's body type. Nicole stated that boys "gravitated" to girls who were curvaceous, which she noted took the attention away from girls who had less body. In an interview with Dee, she explained how she thought boys decided which girls they found attractive regardless of their facial features.

> Tina: Okay, but what about face, does face count?
>
> Dee: Have you ever heard the song "everything look good but her head."
>
> Tina: Huh?
>
> Dee: They [boys] don't care, you ain't gotta look good. You got a body they [boys] going to talk to you. You're not understanding the models are pretty, but they don't want them, they want the body. (Interview, 2008)

Dee determined from her experiences that boys chose their mates for dating based upon on particular criteria required of girls' bodies. For Dee, facial attractiveness, personality, intelligence, or other aesthetics did not concern boys. In a group interview with Lisa and Dee, they further explained how boys treated them because of their body types and identified where these perspectives originated.

> Tina: So do you think Black women on television are represented well?
>
> Lisa: No, not the majority of them because—
>
> Dee: Not these days on Hip Hop videos.
>
> Lisa: Yeah. They look like strippers and hoes.
>
> Tina: How do boys treat you?
>
> Lisa: Most of them think they going get a video girl.
>
> Tina: They do?
>
> Lisa: Some people you hang around in school, yes. They think you supposed to be a certain size, you supposed to wear what they [video girls] wear.
>
> Dee: Yeah, they do.
>
> Lisa: The boys they don't go for librarians or smart girls. Like they wouldn't go for me. They want me to look, you know, what they wanted in the video. Size, strippers dancing, and easy.
>
> Dee: Uh-hm, they want you to look the same way.
>
> Tina: How do you know that?
>
> Lisa: Just the way he act towards you. Like if before you try to talk to them [boys] like we're sitting in the classroom and they know you might like them, they'll say, they'll start talking about, ooh I like that girl because she got that little slim waist and big booty. You know, stuff like that. It just, you already know if he like you, you know you don't look like that, you just step aside. (Interview, 2008)

Dee and Lisa explained the idea that Black boys are only attracted to Black girls who embody a certain size and shape. For the girls, especially the older girls in the study, the idea of being an attractive Black woman centered on body shape. Dee stating that the boys she interacted with did not find smart girls attractive is alarming but speaks to the impact of Hip Hop and its representation of women of color. As referenced in the last chapter, videos like Plies's do not show educated, independent Black women. These videos present women of color as poor and uneducated and, therefore, unable to acquire financial success without trading sex for cash. However, only women who fit a certain body type are given the "privilege" of being chosen by a famous, wealthy male rapper. As a result of Hip Hop's imagery, the boys the girls found attractive did not reciprocate the feelings of attractiveness because the boys wanted girls who mirrored the girls in videos. The girls often expressed frustration with finding a boyfriend. Lara and Lisa at the time of the study had boyfriends. They both informed me that their boyfriends "were good guys." When I asked Lara what she meant by "good guys," she said, "He know better than to be actin' like them other boys" (Interview, 2007).

It is important to note that historically, women of color have debunked mainstream standards of beauty (Lovejoy, 2001). Studies have found that Black girls and women tend to be more content with their body size, weight, and overall appearance when compared to their White counterparts (Akan and Grilo, 1995; Parker et al., 1995; Lovejoy, 2001). Black women are also less likely to develop an eating disorder. I would argue that the young women in the study were confident regarding their bodies; however, they found dissatisfaction with Hip Hop's standards of beauty, which are constructed by both Black and White, male and female, industry workers. The girls in the study found it difficult to date because many of the males they were interested in found girls in videos to be more appealing and sought girls who fit those criteria. To these young women, there is a hidden cost of being a Black girl. Not only did they have to combat the engineered message that essentialized the body of the Black female, but they also found themselves being compared to airbrushed video models who were seen as voluptuous, promiscuous, and perfect.

## Freaks and Hos

When the girls referred to the Black women in videos, they named them *freaks* and *hos*, which are common terms for Black women who appear in rap videos. This industry label is a result of videos showing women with little to nothing on, camera shots that suggest video women are engaging in sex with rappers, and the overall positioning of women of color in videos as sexual objects. The labeling of Black women as freaks has a long history situated within popular culture. It is the unfortunate by-product of the tragic legacy of the Hottentot Venus, who was referred to as a freak but due to racial fetishism was also a sexual object (Hall, 1997). But before Black women appeared in rap videos, they were called Jezebels. According to Stephens and Phillips (2005), White men framed the Jezebel as a woman whose only desire was to please men sexually. Originally, cultural images depicted the Jezebel as a fair-skinned woman with long hair and a shapely body, with emphasis given to her backside. She had an "insatiable sexual appetite" that justified the act of rape by slave masters (Stephens & Phillips, 2005). The archetype of Jezebel laid the foundation for the contemporary sexual script of the Freak that Hip Hop culture and rap music suggest. Stephens and Phillips argue that the Freak is a woman who is "sexually aggressive and wild . . . who simply loves to have sex without any emotional attachment" (p. 20). Her sexual script is that of a woman who has "personal strength" and is "empowered" by her openness to express her sexuality (p. 22). On the other hand, the Freak appears to be following "patriarchal scripts reflecting male defined desires of women's sexuality" (p. 22). Stephens and Phillips suggest that "[t]he everyday usage of these scripts has a direct impact on young African American women's sexual self-concepts, behaviors, and experiences" (p. 35).

The girls, without hesitation or prompting from me, utilized the rhetoric of the patriarchal sexual script to define Black women in rap videos. When I asked the girls how they thought mainstream America represented, and in turn perceived, Black women in videos, they echoed the same response:

> We freaks, we hos, we do anything for money. (Dee, Interview, 2007)
> We be looking like freaks. (Nicole, Interview, 2008)
> They have on their bikinis and stuff in the video, they freaks, they nasty. (Maxine, Interview, 2007)
> Probably that we're [Black women] freaks and we reveal a lot. (Nicole, Interview, 2008)

The use of the word "we" represents a collective notion that dominant culture sees all Black women, regardless of whether they appear in rap videos, as freaks and hos because video models represent Black womanhood to the masses. Thus, the teens in the study saw Black women who appeared in rap videos as freaks and hos with specific biological physical features. The girls felt that the Black women in rap videos, whom they believed allowed the industry to exploit them, were representing all Black women. To the girls, these women set and create the standard for all women of color to follow or resist. The objectification and voyeurism of Hip Hop videos set the stage for Black women to be viewed and analyzed through a variety of socially constructed lenses. The girls' deconstruction of the video women is done without context. These six young women are learning about their world in terms of race, class, sexuality, gender, body, and success through mediated realities, which are made to oppress and exploit them. So before we pass judgment on their interpretations, we have to ask if they ever had a chance to interpret things differently, with what they were given. This is where our coming-of-age stories (mine and theirs) depart, which I will discuss in Chapter Eight. However, before the girls ever hear a demeaning rap lyric or image regarding the Black female body, they hear the intoxicating beat or 808 (drum machine called the Roland TR-808) of Hip Hop music. This beat can paralyze thinking, especially critical thinking. I know this from years of experience. The next chapter illustrates just how powerful the beat of Hip Hop is, as the girls of HCC ignored their better judgment to challenge Hip Hop's misogynistic lyrical content for the sake of the beat.

NEW SOUTH

## *Chapter Seven*

# The Beat of Hegemony

The driving force of Hip Hop is its sound, the beat of the music that pulls you in as a listener. Every rapper knows that in order to have a hit record, the beat of the song must be audibly gratifying for the listener. A rapper's lyrics are secondary to the beat. Before a rapper utters a word, the beat is what pulls the listener into enjoying the song. Hip Hop historians (Forman & Neal, 2004; George, 1999; Rose, 1994) write that the contemporary sound of Hip Hop started in New York City with the arrival of a Jamaican immigrant by the name of Clive Campbell, better known in the Hip Hop world as DJ Kool Herc. Herc grew up with the musical influence of reggae, which infused aspects of African and slave-era music with infectious rhythmic beats (Perkins, 1996). Rose states, "Time suspension via rhythmic breaks—points at which the bass lines are isolated and suspended—are important clues in explaining sources of pleasure in black music" (p. 67). The rhythmic patterns of Hip Hop are powerful, soulful, endearing, and rebellious all at the same time.

The beat of Hip Hop can be both freeing and repressive. For example, in 2005 one of the most hypersexual and misogynistic songs I have ever heard—and liked—was "Wait" by the Ying Yang Twins, an Atlanta-based group. Here is just a small fraction of the foul language within the song: "Fuck a bitch on da counter. . . . Fuck that bend over imma give you the dick. . . . Ay bitch! Wait 'til you see my dick. . . . Beat da pussy up" (Ying Yang Twins, 2005). I was not the only person fond of this song. In 2005, "Wait" reached number two on the *Billboard* charts in the rap category. The video for the song followed the sexist storyline of the record. At one point in the video, there are over twenty half-clothed women laying on top of and around the Ying Yang Twins as they sing "Beat da pussy up." Although I detested the lyrics of the song, the beat was controlling and influential and seemed to paralyze my ability to critically examine the song as it took over my body. Every time I heard the song on the radio or in a club, I thought to myself, "This record is so demeaning to both men and women." However, I was reluctant to turn the song off in my car because I was alone and not visually accountable to anyone for finding pleasure in a song that I knew was misogynistic. This is the contradictory space of Hip Hop feminism, as I was ideologically split by my love for Hip Hop music and culture and my desire to challenge patriarchy. So in an effort to reconcile my divided position as a Hip Hop feminist, I did sit down when the song was played at clubs I attended. This action, in some respect, made me feel both powerful and fake. I took a stand when people were watching, as my social politics were on display, but when I was alone I blasted the song, in love with the beat. Thus, no matter how uncomfortable I felt with the content of the song, the beat kept me drawn to it, and at times I ignored the lyrics. My noncritical position relating to the song, which stopped me from taking personal action to resist it, was common among many of my friends, both male and female. As a collective group, we all knew the song was misogynistic but found it enjoyable.

The teens in the study were no different than my friends and me in regard to enjoying misogynistic rap music. However, as a first-year doctoral student at the time, I was learning to understand rap as a "discourse"—a production of knowledge—and not just as a genre that I found entertaining (Foucault, 1980). Thus, using the words of Foucault and Hall, I began to view rap music and culture as representations that formed issues of power and knowledge and the question of the subject (Hall, 1997). Within rap, the subjects are the rappers and women of color who appear in rap videos, or the women who are cited in rap songs as bitches. Yet, according to Foucault, subjects are not autonomous and stable entities; subjects are produced within the "regime of truth," which operates by creating truths that are discursive, which in turn regulates social practices and what is deemed as knowledge and power (Foucault, 1980). For example, there is much discourse surrounding same-sex parents' inability to effectively parent. There is no evidence that this assumption is accurate. On the contrary, there are a good number of studies that contend that same-sex parents are effective parents (Pruett & Pruett, 2009). Nonetheless, the common discourse penalizes same-sex parents and gives power to heterosexual parents. This position that leads individuals to give truth and power to discursive information is what Italian theorist Antonio Gramsci called hegemony. McLaren (1994) defines hegemony as "a struggle in which the powerful win the consent of those who are oppressed, with the oppressed unknowingly participating in their own oppression. . . . Within the hegemonic process, established meanings are often laundered of contradiction, contestation, and ambiguity" (pp. 182–183). By way of Foucault and Hall, I was learning how to be media literate. Thus, media literacy gave me the control to resist songs like "Wait" and its hegemonic message, which I struggled to disrupt.

But I was twenty-five years old with two degrees and working toward a third before I understood hegemony and its fluidity regarding Black popular culture. I never learned in high school that Hip Hop music and culture had been co-opted to create music and sounds that only highlighted the most demeaning notions of Blackness. As a youngster and young adult, I unknowingly consented to hypersexual, degrading, and misogynistic lyrics of rap. My consent often led to contradictory thinking, as I opposed the same music whose beat I enjoyed. My experience was no different than the girls in the study. Sad to say, it took a Ph.D. program to teach me media literacy.

## The Beat Goes on . . .

Similar to my experiences with the beat of rap, the problematic lyrics and images of rap music were secondary to the beat of the music for the girls, even as the girls critiqued the music for its derogatory content, which is highlighted in Chapter Eight. In "Keepin' It Real: Black Youth, Hip-Hop Culture, and Black Identity," Clay (2003) recognized that "in conversations, many of the youth said that it was the 'beats,' not the lyrics, that are important to them about hip-hop" (p. 1346). Many of the teens in this study echoed Clay's findings that the beat drove them to listen to and accept degrading lyrics.

> They [male rappers] call us the "H" stuff and you get kind of offended, but I don't know why. We still listen and dance because we like the beat. (Star, Interview, 2007)

> When I first heard it [Plies, "Shawty]," I listened to the whole song. Then I just start laughing. I was like, he nasty. And like now . . . I didn't listen to it, I listen to the beat. (Nicole, Interview, 2007)

> You listen to it and if a boy come up to me and I like the song, and I can turn it off. (Lisa, Interview, 2007)

The teens referred to the beat for enjoyment, disregarding the messages, which is problematic because the music's messages take on a latent, secondary meaning in juxtaposition to the primacy of the beat. As the girls found pleasure in rap music because of the beat, they consented to degrading diatribes about Black culture and Black identity even as they brilliantly critiqued it. I read their consent to the misogynistic and sexually explicit lyrics as revealing a hegemonic structure at play within rap music and Black popular culture. Although the girls denounced the sexist lyrics by attempting to ignore them, they still danced and listened to the songs. Furthermore, the girls created methods of reconciling the contradictory space because they knew listening to the songs sent a message to their male counterparts regarding sex, which was a message the girls wanted to control. However, the beat of the songs made the girls disregard their better judgment.

For example, Lisa admitted that she would not listen to degrading songs if a male was present; this is insightful. Lisa feared that males would think she was promiscuous, which could have social ramifications. Her intuitive refusal to listen to sexually explicit rap music around males illustrates the complex world in which she lived, as she enjoyed the beat of rap by herself or with her girlfriends but knew the unspoken ramifications for listening to explicit rap with males. Lisa knew that males would label her a freak or a ho, much like the women in videos. Nevertheless, by listening to the song, Lisa consented to the message. Maxine too realized that male rappers degraded Black women in rap songs. Just like Lisa, however, she listened to the songs because of the beat. Nicole stated that she does not even listen to the lyrics of "Shawty" by Plies—she just listened to the beat of the song. "Shawty" is one of Plies's hit records, and the title track topped the *Billboard* charts for rap tracks. In the song, Plies states, "I told her I don't usually do this, I don't fuck on the first night, 'cause after I beat ya baby I'm liable to fuck up ya whole life. I gotta train her, now she suck me with ice" (Plies, 2007). Nicole knew that the song was vulgar, so she only listened for the beat. Nicole was not alone; Dee and Maxine also admitted that they did not know the song lyrics and at times only knew the chorus but enjoyed the beat.

> So you don't think about it at all, just the beat. (Dee, Interview, 10/07)
>
> I don't like it, I just. I don't like it, I like the beat. I just don't like the fact that he's talking about it and all that. Like Soulja Boy—I like Soulja Boy—The real version is not good. I don't like it because it's talking about sex . . . um, degrading women. (Maxine, Interview, 2007)

Dee admitted that she does not think about the degrading lyrics because she knows how damaging the lyrics are. Her love of the beat superseded her position that the music was problematic. Above, Maxine referenced Soulja Boy's hit song "Crank Dat." In the song Soulja Boy states, "Super soak that hoe. I'm too fresh off in this bitch. . . . And superman that bitch." "Crank Dat" is yet another song with an infectious beat and a memorable chorus but problematic lyrics. To "superman" a woman is to masturbate and then ejaculate on the back of a female. Maxine understood the coded language of the record, so she preferred to listen to the song for the beguiling beat.

All the girls liked to dance. Because it was a community center that focused on homework help, the environment restricted much of the music to their personal mp3 players or iPods. Therefore, the girls would pass around their mp3 players so everyone could hear the latest dance songs. Maxine spoke passionately about her dislike of rap music because of how it degrades women. When I asked her if she liked Soulja Boy's song "Crank Dat," she repeated the phrase, "I don't like it." Maxine tried to resist rap's message when the songs degraded women. At times during our interviews, Maxine told me that she refused to listen to music by Soulja Boy that was sexually explicit. According to my observations, though, Maxine's resistance was not consistent, much like mine as I enjoyed the Ying Yang Twins.

> Maxine loves to dance. She and Star know all the latest dances including the Soulja Boy, who has become extremely popular. Even though Maxine has stated she does not like Soulja Boy, she and Star dance to the song every time one of the students has it on their mp3 players. (Field notes, B. Love, 1/08)

My field notes and observations addressed many of the students' conflicted and contradictory ideological stances. Maxine wanted rap music to change. She stated that she did not like rap music that degrades women and is sexually explicit, but she continued to use Soulja Boy as a medium for social engagement. Emerson (2002) argues that sexually explicit music "limits the autonomy and agency of Black women" (p. 120). When Maxine danced to Soulja Boy, she contradicted her dislike for misogynistic rap music. Therefore, her participation led to her consent to the music. Maxine's and the rest of the girls' consent to find enjoyment in some of rap's most debasing messages is an example of hegemony, as the girls, a marginalized group, consented to their own oppression. Storey (1998) stated that the relationship between popular culture and hegemony is the "site of struggle between the forces of 'resistance' of subordinate groups in society, and the forces of 'incorporation' of dominant groups in society" (p. 14).

The girls stated that they found the lyrics of rap music explicit and vulgar; however, their cell phone ring tones were the same songs they detested. They consumed rap in multiple ways—cell phones, mp3 players, radio, videos, and the Internet. Each Internet music site provided the beat to the music in which they escaped while doing their homework or searching the Internet.

Some of my field notes address the beat of the music as a vital part of their day at the center.

> Dee and Lisa did their homework while listening to music today. They would bob their heads while doing their homework humming the beat of the song. They would smile at certain parts of the song and sometimes smile at each other. (Field notes, B. Love, 2007)

The beat served as the background for many of their daily activities, especially homework. I observed students' dancing at times with no music playing, just the beat they carried in their heads. They hummed the beat as they danced. I witnessed students dancing from the computer lab to the homework station, even when they did not have a portable music player. They identified with the beat of the music first; the lyrics really were an afterthought. The girls hummed the beat because they knew the words were not appropriate at the center and often times they did not even know all the words to the song. However, the beat was a fundamental part of their daily activities.

The beat influenced a resounding number of comments, which led the youth to consent blindly to the messages. Even when the youth expressed their dislike for the lyrics, the beat of the music kept them listening.

> It's just they cute. Like I don't know, I listen to the songs because I think how cute they is but they've got some songs on there that's nice, they're nice. I like the beat and stuff. (Lara, Interview, 2007)

> Yeah, but I don't like the words, I like the beat. . . . Sometimes you don't understand what they be saying, so fast. (Maxine, Interview, 2007)

Obviously, the teens maintained that the beat of a song was the driving force behind why they listened to the song. Yet, they acknowledged the presence of the lyrics. They explained that they did not know many of the words to a particular song and may not have liked the particular rapper but enjoyed the beat. Adams and Fuller (2006) argued, "It is imperative that we as a society move beyond the beat and seriously consider the effect that negative imagery produced in misogynistic rap can have on the African American community and society at large" (p. 955). The beat of the song masks the explicit lyrics of rap music and the negative imagery consumed by youth who enjoy the songs. Because the youth engaged with the beat, their ability to evaluate the lyrics was challenged.

## Nobody Wants to Be Lame

The girls in the study were at the age where being accepted by their peers was extremely important. Hip Hop music and culture were precursors to their peers' accepting them. The girls believed there were social ramifications for not liking the rap music of their peers or taking a stand against music they found to be demeaning. The girls conceptualized rap's vulgar language as a permanent fixture within rap and feared being seen as lame or as someone who thought otherwise. When I asked Dee why she listened to music she thought was belittling to women she stated, "What can I do, it's everywhere you go" (Dee, informal interview, 2008). Dee is right; in Atlanta music that has a sexual message can be heard just about everywhere. Moreover, if the lyrics cannot be heard, the beat is in the background. To be clear, I am not an advocate of censoring music that has sexual messages; I support the need for girls and boys to learn the tools to unpack sexual and degrading messages regarding women and hyper-macho stereotypes of masculinity. Furthermore, if students, no matter their gender, had a space in schools to collectively resist messages from popular culture, regardless if it's Hip Hop or not, they would be more apt to resist those messages outside of schools.

Young girls need a space where they feel comfortable resisting demeaning notions of womanhood. They also need teachers who expose popular culture for its contrived messages built on stereotypes but do not demoralize youth choices to consume Hip Hop or any form of popular culture; this is a hard pedagogical technique but is needed, according to the experiences of the girls. For example, Lisa commented on the social repercussions associated with attempts to take action against the music when I asked her why she does not turn off songs she believes degrade women. Lisa stated, "If you say turn it off, then you lame" (Lisa, informal interview, 2008). Previously, Lisa had stated that she does not listen to sexually explicit music around males; however, here she has a fear of being viewed as uncool by her peers for turning off the music. Lisa wants to live above the peer pressure but does not know how, which is evident by her words. Lisa is at odds because she is trying to fit in and take a stance in spaces that are overwhelmed with the music she is trying to challenge. Nicole passionately speculated, "Everyone dances to the music, how would it look if you don't dance"? (Nicole, informal interview, 2008). None of the girls ever tried resisting rap's misogynistic and sexually explicit lyrics by participating in some type of social action. In contrast, I resisted misogynistic rap music in public spaces because of my peer group and a fear of not being seen as socially conscious but did not resist when I was alone. However, when I was sixteen, I remember being at a club screaming at the top of my lungs to Akinyele's song "Put It in Your Mouth." In the song, Akinyele raps, "What do ya choose to lick you could eat me out pussy or dick? Put it in your mouth" (Akinyele, 1996). I enjoyed this song for the beat and the lyrics. Some of the lyrics I really did not understand at the time, but, most importantly, everyone at the club seemed to like it, so that was my clue to like the song as well. I was only sixteen and not old enough to be at the club, but my older friends got me in. I did not want to seem straitlaced or not excited about the song along with my peers, and I genuinely liked the song. I still do. However, now I can enjoy it, critically deconstruct it, and not fear what my peers may think of my ideological positions. My fear, like that of the girls, is best explained by Freire's notion of fear of freedom. On this topic he wrote (2000):

> The oppressed, having internalized the image of the oppressor and adopted his guidelines, are fearful of freedom. Freedom would require them to reject this image and replace it with autonomy and responsibility. . . . However, the oppressed, who have adapted to the structure of domination in which they are immersed, and have become resigned to it, are inhibited from waging the struggle for freedom so long as they feel incapable of running the risk it requires. (p. 47)

The pressure to conform to what society and rap music say Black men and women should be like is quite powerful and hegemonic. The girls and I feared the risk of being uncool—or to use Lisa's term, lame—if we rejected misogynistic rap music. Therefore, we enjoyed the beat and ignored our better judgment because of the fear of being an outcast. Fear was the driving force of our conformity; we wanted to fit in and be seen as cool. Learning the latest dance and listening to the most popular rap song were the cool things to do, and none of the girls, including myself years ago, felt powerful enough to resist Hip Hop's misogynistic messages. Although the girls succumbed to the pressure of Hip Hop's contentious messages about Black women and what it means to be a Black woman, they found space to resist messages regarding Black men. It is also important to note that sexual songs can be pleasurable, which makes misogynistic rap music even harder to resist. However, young girls must be able to critique and decode the messages of rap, alongside its sexual seduction. Furthermore, the girls were not yet able to examine self and messages of Black female identity but were keen in deconstructing the media and Hip Hop for its portrayal of Black males.

## *Chapter Eight*

# Black Girls Resisting When No One Is Listening

Intuitively, the girls resisted Hip Hop's more pugnacious messages. A fundamental part of consuming popular culture is resisting popular culture. Hall (1981) argued, "Popular culture is one of the sites where this struggle for and against culture of the powerful is engaged: it is also the stake to be won or lost in the struggle. It is the arena of consent and resistance" (p. 65). I, however, argue that their resistance was undermined by rap's hegemonic force, which can be a normal outcome in today's mass media built on hegemonic race, class, gender, and political ideologies. Collins (2004) writes:

> All women engage an ideology that deems middle-class, heterosexual, White femininity as normative. In this context, Black femininity as a subordinated gender identity becomes constructed not just in relation to White women, but also in relation to multiple others, namely, all men, sexual outlaws (prostitutes and lesbians), unmarried women, and girls. These benchmarks construct a discourse of a hegemonic (White) femininity that becomes a normative yardstick for all femininities in which Black women typically are relegated to the bottom of the gender hierarchy. (p. 193)

The girls' resistance was never nurtured in classrooms, where conversations that problematize and critique rap in nonjudgmental disclosures took place, which are vital to their development. Their voices and experiences with rap were disregarded in classrooms and pushed to the margins. The complex issues of race, sexuality, class, and gender that are embedded within the music are dismissed by school officials as immature youth culture and music not worthy of classroom time. When I began to ask the girls to critique Hip Hop, their intellectual prowess was evident. The girls understood that the music did not always represent Black folks in constructive ways, specifically Black men, and that the messages within rap were problematic.

> Like they need to change what they talking about. They [rappers] probably not like that for real but they know that young people don't do that and want to sing it and stuff because of the beat and stuff and they doing it mostly because of money. . . . Future kids that doing drugs, so they're sending out future things so what the police and the government and the President is doing, building more jailhouses than schools and after school because people are going to drop out, they know people are going to drop out and go to jail. (Maxine, Interview, 2007)

> Like violence. Like they [rappers] be talking about how they got guns and then you know a teenager might think they can have guns, they [rappers] go get a gun to feel protected. They [rappers] talk about they might want to go to jail then come rap about how they was in jail. You know, like they be some of them songs have a negative impact on children because they want to be just like the rappers. (Lisa, Interview, 2007)

> Yeah, talking about killing people and stuff (Lara, Interview, 2007)

These comments make it apparent that the girls had the ability to negotiate not only rap but also social issues around the music and urban life. Maxine's notions that rap needs to change and her understandings of the social issues that plague the Black community were insightful in that she used contemporary politics to address some of the current sociopolitical issues Black America faces. The fact that Maxine thought in regard to future generations showed her keen intellect and concern for others. Maxine also understood the masked racism of the prison industrial complex. Moreover, the girls' comments about violence represented their ideological perspectives concerning rappers and gun use. Lisa linked rappers' gun use to the belief that rappers carrying guns may influence other youth to follow their example. Dyson (2007) stated, "There's a preoccupation with the gun because the gun is the central part of the iconography of the ghetto" (p. 91). Black youth's obsession with guns and violence, according to Dyson, is a staple of urban life. Lisa linked guns and violence to rap music and rappers. She spoke to the perpetual violence that takes place in urban communities because of the belief that males need a gun to be viewed as fully masculine. Lisa understood the large-scale significance of rap music.

When I asked the girls why they thought rappers rhymed about guns and violence, they all stated in some fashion that rappers do not care about the youth who listen to their music.

> It is all about money basically. They [rappers] really don't care. Oh, they're [rappers] sending a bad message. (Lara, Interview, 2008)

> They don't care about us. They care about that money. (Star, Interview, 2008)

> They do it for money. (Nicole, Interview, 2008)

The girls state that rappers take on hardcore and hypersexual facades for financial gain. Their critique of rap speaks to the materialistic, bling-bling culture of the music that glorifies conspicuous consumption above social issues that many scholars have unpacked (Basu, 2005; Love, 2010). A more concrete example surrounding the girls' thoughts regarding rappers and their motives lies in their opinions of Atlanta-based rapper T.I. (Clifford Joseph Harris, Jr.) and his hardcore image. During the study, the police arrested T.I. on federal gun charges. A few of the girls referred to T.I. as an example of poor decision making, as a negative role model for youth, and as forging a criminal image to profit financially. Prior to his arrest, T.I. was a local hero. T.I. represented the city of Atlanta to the rest of America when he starred in the movie *A.T.L.*, a coming-of-age story set in Atlanta that was a mainstream success and grossed over $21.1 million. Before T.I's fall from grace, he was producing, song writing, and launching his own movie company. The teens, however, expressed disappointment in T.I. and his gangster image, which led to his spending one year and a day in prison.

> Not T.I., he got locked up. T.I., I like him but he is a bad influence so that's it. Because he's in jail. And what he did wasn't called for. Like he shouldn't have did it. . . . And he got everybody disappointed, all his fans and stuff. . . . Now that he's going to do time because he's in jail, he gone be there a while. (Star, Interview, 2008)

> Something wrong with that boy; he think he tough. (Dee, Interview, 2008)

> He actin' like that for money. (Lara, Interview, 2008)

Star spoke about her disappointment that T.I. was possibly going to jail. Her disappointment demonstrated that she liked T.I. prior to his gun charges and felt saddened by his poor judgment. She understood T.I.'s gun charge as a collapse of his career. The fact that many of the girls questioned T.I.'s image and reasons for making records showed they were aware of and concerned with the message within T.I.'s music. The teens did not applaud T.I.'s fall from greatness that resulted from his criminal activity. Star looked upon T.I.'s message of violence and criminal activity as discreditable, and the fact that the rapper's stage persona became a reality disappointed her. Lara suggested that money was the primary reason for T.I.'s hardcore image. In an interview with Lisa, she accused T.I. of pretending to be dangerous and nefarious to sell records.

> Lisa: He actin' like that to sell records.
>
> Tina: Actin' like what?
>
> Lisa: Like he a gangsta. Actin' hard. (Interview, 2008)

Similar to Lara's claims, Lisa questioned the authenticity of T.I.'s pugnacious image. The girls felt T.I.'s words and lifestyle, which compose his rap persona, were a sham. The girls critically examined the authenticity of T.I. and his music. These examinations of T.I., and Hip Hop music and culture in general, are important to the overall growth and well-being of Black girls and all youth. The dialogue that these girls engaged in created a space for them to resist rap's monolithic image of Black males.

However, conversations surrounding Black women did not produce the same outcome. When I asked the girls to examine Black women with a more critical lens, they relied heavily on how Black women react to the position of Black males. For example, Maxine felt that Black women dressed scantily in rap videos because they were attempting to gain the attention of males. Lisa, Dee, and Lara had views parallel to those of Maxine. The girls felt that Black women's choices were a reaction to what Black males wanted, as well as poor decision making in general. Conversely, the teens saw rap through multiple lenses of Black expression. In some cases the teens challenged rap's hegemonic messages, but in other cases the teens understood rap as essentialized notions of Blackness and were unable to reject its images and sounds. Their conflicting stances and positions on rap music might be explained through what Phillips (2006) called the "postmodern condition" (p. 1). Phillips (2006) defined the postmodern condition as

> cultural hybridizations and mestizaje, combined with global Westernization; moral indeterminism; the increasing impact of simulacra on psychological processes; and the increasing indeterminacy or complexity of identity. (p. 1)

Phillips's definition of the postmodern condition is the reality in which we all live. Black popular culture, among many other factors, influences identity, which is complex. Identity is a hybrid of multiple constructions of self, and for these Black girls, Black popular culture was the most influential popular subculture. Therefore, the postmodern condition made it possible for Black girls to critique rap and, at the same time, condone, enjoy, and find pleasure in its messages. When asked about what they thought it meant to be Black, all the youth stated that to be Black is to be beautiful, smart, athletic, and have the ability to dance. They essentialized their ideas of what it means to be Black on multiple levels depending on the question. The data showed that the teens contradicted themselves as they struggled to make meaning of images of Blackness that they understood as authentic, even when those images glorified degrading women. The teens resisted labeling the Black race as violent, but they accepted Black women who appeared in rap videos as hos and freaks. The postmodern condition allows these fluid and contradictory ideas because of the hybridizations of culture and the contradictory nature of Black popular culture (Hall, 1983). Their conclusions regarding the choices of Black women, discussed throughout this book, illustrate why Black girls need a space to question what it means to be a Black woman in conjunction with how Hip Hop, issues of class, race, politics, and body influence Black womanhood.

The data expressed within this book show that girls are engaging in the complicated and contradictory work of negotiating the space of Hip Hop music and culture but are doing the work alone. The girls were able to deconstruct Hip Hop's violent images in profound ways and question the lyrical content of rappers as juxtaposed to their own lives. Also, through questioning rappers' authenticity, the girls interrogated the monolithic image of male rappers as hardcore. Their critiques are insightful and have the power to become the foundation of revolutionary change and paradigm shifts in youth culture; however, these teens found no educational support to explore further rap's contrived and stereotypical messages.

Urban classrooms that are centered on urban youth must be classrooms that are also centered on culturally relevant pedagogy with its foundation in Hip Hop music and culture. When urban schools choose to ignore their students' culture they are creating buildings where students do not feel connected to education because the curriculum is foreign to them. Teaching through a Hip Hop-inspired pedagogical and media literacy approach is culturally responsive pedagogy with possibilities for social action in that teaching through a culturally relevant framework is restructuring classroom politics (Emdin, 2010b). If the six girls within this study experienced culturally responsive pedagogy rooted in Hip Hop that integrated media literacy skills, they would have been able to question the racist and sexist messages in the music that led them to believe that women of color were inferior to White women. It was difficult for the girls to understand Hip Hop music and culture as racist and sexist because, to them, Black women enter a fair and equal workforce. The girls also experienced how rap's messages impacted them in their everyday lives in terms of dating, body, and attracting males who attended their schools.

This book offers a glimpse into the complex lives of six girls who are sisters, daughters, granddaughters, cousins, and friends of people who impacted their lives and whom I never met. What this book does show, simply, is a need for media literacy, Hip Hop pedagogy and feminism, and a counter to the attack waged by corporate America against our daughters via Hip Hop music and culture. Times have changed and schools have to change with it or they will fail to educate. That is why I wrote this book. I can remember sitting in class as a teenager asking myself whether anyone cared about what was going on in my community besides my friends and me. I recall thinking to myself that KRS-One knew more about me, my community, and my history as an African American than did my teachers, regardless of race, whom I saw every day. These thoughts left me disconnected from school. I often hear older Black folks profess that today's youth are lost. When older generations of Black folks scrutinize rap music, they fail to recognize the impact technology has on today's youth and on society as a whole. To put this claim in perspective and illustrate some of the similarities and differences between my generation and the current generation, in the next section I travel back to my childhood and my interactions with the music and culture of Hip Hop.

### **"Analog Girl in a Digital World"** — *Erykah Badu*

One year for Christmas, I got a radio/boombox that had a black and white T.V. built into it. After the excitement of unwrapping my boombox, my parents told me they forgot to buy batteries. The radio took about sixteen batteries. So on Christmas day in Rochester, New York, where temperatures can reach below zero, I took my radio, covered in a garbage bag, and enough money to purchase sixteen batteries to the corner store. My parents watched me the entire time in fear that someone might steal my radio. When I got home I put the batteries in my radio and blasted Rochester's local radio station. I then played my tapes (or should I say my brother's tapes that I stole from him). Lastly, I twisted the switch on the boombox that turned on the T.V.—I could not play both at the same time. I only got three fuzzy T.V. stations on my radio, and when the batteries died so did the radio. My parents were not going to give me money every week or so to buy sixteen batteries. So my radio became a piece of art in my room—Hip Hop memorabilia. More important, when my radio died my access to music died with it. Like many families, we had a radio in our home, but it was my parents' radio, so James Brown, Sam Cooke, and Bobby "Blue" Bland were the sounds of home. I had no money to buy tapes or call in a video on The Box. The Box was a television station that charged its viewers to play music videos. A caller would call a pay-per-call number, select the videos they wanted to see by number and be billed from $1.99 to $3.99. Before MTV this was the only way to watch rap videos. In 1999, MTV bought The Box network. This all may sound ancient to younger folks, but finding Hip Hop music is part of the Hip Hop generation's story. Most Hip Hop was underground, in part because no one who looked like me had any money to buy music, and if someone could afford to buy music, most record stores did not carry many copies of rap albums or did not allow in buyers without a parent; record stores essentially policed what youth could buy and hear. We relied on our friends to make a copy of an album, which typically was a copy of a copy. Once we got the copy, the sound quality was so bad that we could barely hear the rapper's lyrics. This is my memory of Hip Hop: the quest to have access to the music. In those early days, listening to Hip Hop was quite intimate. It was just me or my friends, the artist, and the beat.

Perhaps most salient for this book in regard to my childhood is the fact that I was virtually able to dress, think, and act in any way I liked as a young girl. When acts like De La Soul, A Tribe Called Quest, Monie Love, and Queen Latifah emerged wearing dashikis, African headwraps, and kente prints and promoting love, individuality, and respect for one's self and community, I was hooked. However, there were artists whom I loved that were more provocative, like Slick Rick, who released his 1988 debut album entitled "The Great Adventures of Slick Rick" featuring songs entitled "Treat Her Like a Prostitute" and "Lick the Balls." My first Hip Hop concert was LL Cool J. My mother took me to the concert but happily escorted me out of the show when LL started making sex motions on a couch that he had on stage as he sang the song "I Need Love." I also listened to Public Enemy, who criticized America's race relations, economics, media, politics, and treatment of people of color. But I adored N.W.A (Niggaz Wit Attitudes), who rapped "Fuck the Police" because of police brutality and introduced me to oral sex with the song "She Swallowed It." My generation had access to all types of Hip Hop music. We could choose to imitate rappers who rapped about politics, police corruption and brutality, African ancestral roots, racism, and uplifting the poor, along with sex, drugs, crime, and verbally assaulting women. The reason behind this diversity was simple: Hip Hop represented a wide range of ideas and experiences held by Black and Brown folks. There was no monolithic Black voice. At this time, corporate America did not determine what it meant to be a person of color marginalized by mainstream culture, because corporate America did not see Hip Hop as profitable yet or as a threat to White America. Before mainstream America took control of Hip Hop music and culture, the genre depicted multiple viewpoints of Black life because it was under the radar of corporate thugs. In my teenage years, rap music and culture represented the breadth and scope of Black life. Since there is no one way to be Black, there was no one Hip Hop sound or image. Today's rap music is saturated with one type of Hip Hop sound—that most profitable and acceptable to Whites' eyes and ears. Comparing the messages within rap between when I grew up and now, the lyrical content is not that much different. In juxtaposing Slick Rick's and N.W.A.'s lyrics to Lil' Wayne or Kanye West, one sees that there are more similarities than differences. So if the music has not significantly changed in the last thirty years, what has? I would argue access and the industry. Music that questions society in terms of racism, sexism, classism, and xenophobic attitudes is rarely heard on popular radio stations and T.V. stations that air rap videos. Therefore, Black youth have limited access to rap music and images that celebrate the multiple and varying identities of Black life, but unlimited access to the trope of Black females as sex objects who are uneducated, promiscuous, and poor decision makers.

My love for Hip Hop music is no different than that of Lara, Dee, Star, Maxine, Nicole, and Lisa, but my access to the music and the musical options differ. My struggle as a youth living in a broken home mimics many of the girls' homes. Just like Hip Hop past and present, the girls and I have many similarities. Even though my sexuality and location are different from those of the young ladies in this study, we all grew up as young women who turned to Black popular culture for answers and identity cues. Let's be real: Misogyny, hypersexuality, and promiscuity in Hip Hop music did not start with Lil' Wayne or Jay-Z. Women as sexual props have always been part of Black music, part of America. However, generations prior to the digital age had narrow contact with Black popular culture, and that culture was created more at the community level. To be clear, the music industry did not start exploiting Black artists with the emergence of rap; the industry has always exploited people of color, but previously the industry did not have the capabilities to stream, download, Google, and make an app into images and sounds that send ideas of White supremacy to Black youth. The girls in this study were in the beginning stages of questioning rap. On their own, they were engaging in Hip Hop pedagogy and resisting representations that labeled Black males as bellicose. However, they did it alone. According to Rose (2008), "Members of the hip hop generation are now facing the greatest media machinery and most veiled forms of racial, economic, sexual and gender rhetoric in modern history; they need the sharpest critical tools to survive and thrive" (p. 9). In order for youth to survive and thrive, as Rose points out, education must prepare them for the intellectual fight of their lives, because our youth are under attack.

## Controlled Choice

Youth of color consume more T.V. and videos than do their White counterparts. Black youth watch images that celebrate Black men and women for violent behavior, drug use, hypersexuality, and, most dangerously, being uneducated. Black youth engage with popular culture where sexism, racism, and stereotyping are the norm. Countless commercials fill the airwaves that transmit images of Black women speaking with stereotypical "Black" inflections as dreamed up in the White imagination. Television ads show Black men as hypermasculine and aggressive. And T.V. shows like *Real Housewives of Atlanta*, *Basketball Wives*, and *Love & Hip Hop Atlanta* represent Black women to the masses as loud, ignorant, violent, and incapable of having a husband, as only a few of the wives are actually married. Corporate America bombards Black youth of both genders—at the crucial stage of adolescence where identity exploration develops—with propaganda that demeans people of color.

Cultivation theory (Brown, 1993; Gerbner, Gross, Morgan, & Signorielli, 1994) suggests that frequent viewing increases the likelihood of adopting the values and beliefs expressed by the content to which one is exposed. Gruber and Thau (2003) stated that when researchers apply cultivation theory to children they notice that the perspectives forwarded in media representations increase the rate of adopting beliefs that result in behavior changes. Social learning theory (Bandura, 1989; Ward & Rivadeneyra, 1999) contends that people learn by observing others and that the observers will ultimately practice those learned behaviors. Social learning theory research also supports the hypothesis that videos shape the minds and actions of our youth (Brown, 1993; Ward & Rivadeneyra, 1999). These two theories are central to my findings in the research on the girls, who have unlimited access to the contrived space of Black popular culture. Thus, the conclusions that these six girls surmised from their context are exactly the conclusions that corporate America poured billions of dollars into achieving. These girls are not dumb or dopes; they are using their social, cultural, and educational context to inform their world. Moreover, rap's contrived messages that use Black faces to undermine Black empowerment set the compelling stage for a generation plagued by joblessness, unplanned pregnancies, drugs, criminal activity, and terrifyingly high rates of HIV infections (Collins, 2004). If we, as educators, community leaders, parents, and policy makers, are to counter the corporate-manipulated space of Black popular culture, we must teach our youth how to be media literate. I am convinced that the music industry will not change—it is not in their financial interest to do so. But how we educate our youth can change. Media literacy and Hip Hop pedagogy have to become a part of Black girls' lives as well as the lives of all youth.

## Hip Hop Pedagogy Reimagined

> Students may very well have ideas and insights that adults are not privy to and could prove to be very helpful to improving schools if adults were willing to listen.
>
> —Pedro Noguera (2008, p. 69)

Books on education and youth typically end with suggestions and grandiose recommendations. I think educational recommendations are important, but I hope to close with what I know works based on my personal experiences as a teacher and a teacher educator. Like any art form, Hip Hop has its flaws, but there is an indisputable power in the words of those artists who exercise such influence over our youth on a daily basis. It is precisely because rap discusses controversial issues like sex, violence, drugs, and homophobia that we must use rap to bring these issues to the forefront in schools. We cannot acknowledge the profound impact rap music has upon our youth and yet continue to disregard its potential; in doing so, we are ignoring the culture of our youth. Today's classrooms must engage students in ways that link students' lives and communities to their education and make it meaningful. What I am describing is culturally relevant pedagogy. This is why culturally relevant pedagogy is rooted in what Ladson-Billings and Tate (1995) call "good teaching," and it involves three components: academic achievement, cultural competence, and sociopolitical competence. These three components compose Hip Hop pedagogy.

Pough (2004) argues that when we listen to rap and use it as a discussion tool, it can help students consciously and radically challenge and "break apart the racial, political, sexual, and economic prejudices that listeners bring when they hear rap" (p. 195). Discussing rap music in the classroom does not promote sex or drug use; it is a chance to explore why rap is filled with these images and how racism and sexism flood the music (Pough, 2004). We should integrate individuals—like Childish Gambino, Mos Def, Jay-Z, David Banner, Goodie Mob, Jean Grae, Lil' Wayne, Phonte, Lupe Fiasco, Jay Electronica, T.I, Tiye Phoenix, OutKast, Lauryn Hill, Meduse, B.O.B, KRS-One, and Dead Prez—and the issues they raise into classroom curriculum. These artists and their music can give youth multiple perspectives of modern Black America. For example, Lauryn Hill's social justice music mixed with the gritty street sounds of Jay-Z can present a fuller picture of Black America and assist youth in becoming informed critical consumers of rap (Steinberg, 2007). Also, we cannot forget that Hip Hop pedagogy is comprised of all the elements of Hip Hop, not just rap. Hip Hop pedagogy recognizes and celebrates how youth move, speak, think, create, and relate to the world. A classroom that embodies Hip Hop pedagogy is filled with movement, love, and freedom of expression. In teaching, the most important consideration of all is creating a classroom where students have knowledge of self, their community, and love for each other. Hip Hop pedagogy is crucial because Lipsitz (1994) reminds us that "if we fail to locate them [youth] with the racialized social crisis of our time . . . our understanding of that crisis will also be incomplete if we fail to learn the lesson that young people are trying to teach through dance, dress, speech, and visual imaging" (p. 18). Youth bring unique experiences into the classroom. We as teachers must tap into Hip Hop's potential in order to re-imagine how all the elements of Hip Hop can be used as classroom tools, instead of treating them as the elephant in the room.

Critical media literacy is another pedagogical approach that educators can utilize in the classroom in conjunction with Hip Hop pedagogy to expand students' understanding of racism, sexism, and the media's manufactured marketing of stereotypes (Kellner & Share, 2007). Critical media literacy helps students "critically analyze relationships between media and audiences, information, and power" (Kellner & Share, 2007, p. 4). In this way, students can begin to create their own ideas about gender, race, class, and power as they challenge the media's formulaic representations of these constructs (Kellner & Share, 2007; Torres & Mercado, 2007). Lewis and Jhally (1998) stated that "the goal of media literacy is to help people become sophisticated citizens rather than sophisticated consumers" (p. 109). The primary objective of critical media literacy is to create counter representations or alternative perspectives of the media and thus promote civic participation and social change. As a participatory, collaborative exploration of the media, critical media literacy is a transformative process for both the students and educators (Kellner, 1998; Kellner & Share, 2007). With this method, the teacher is not simply criticizing the music or the culture of the students but also helping all parties involved to examine their own assumptions (Freire, 2000; Kellner & Share, 2007; Steinberg, 2007). As this study illustrates, there is a dire need for educational policy that focuses on a curriculum inclusive of critical media literacy. Kellner and Share argued (2007) that implementing critical media literacy is not an option in today's multimedia world and in an educational system driven by standardized high-stakes testing: The implementation of critical media literacy is necessary to empower students "to create their own messages that can challenge media texts and narratives" (p. 60). Ashcraft (2006) argues, in particular, for a critical pedagogy that includes the critique of popular culture texts in order to best engage students in the critique of discourses of gender, race, class, and sexuality. Burbules and Berk (1999) pointed out that "critical pedagogy authors would argue that by helping to make people more critical in thought and action, progressively minded educators can help to free learners to see the world as it is and to act accordingly; critical education can increase freedom and enlarge the scope of human possibilities" (p. 1). There is a lack of development of critical thinking skills throughout the educational system. Giroux (2003) suggested that our nation's schools are

> bereft of financial support and confronted by myriad problems that include overcrowded classrooms, crumbling school buildings, chronic shortages of classroom materials, demoralized teachers, and budget shortfalls. Many of the nation's schools are in dire straits and can no longer provide a decent, quality education, especially to those children who live in poor rural or urban areas. (p. 72)

These issues impede the learning process and prevent students from developing the skills to become critical of rap music. The current educational system fails to empower urban youth because it does not encourage them to be critical of Hip Hop. Giroux (1988) argued that the aim of the critical educator should be "to raise ambitions, desires, and real hope for those who wish to take seriously the issue of educational struggle and social justice" (p. 177). The Black girls at HCC struggled with their ambitions and desires in the face of rap music, racism, and sexism.

According to Giroux, the educational system has the same fears as society has of students of color. Giroux (2003) explained this fear adeptly.

> Schools increasingly resemble prisons, and students begin to look more like criminal suspects who need to be searched, tested, and observed under the watchful eye of administrators who appear to be less concerned with educating them than with policing their every move. Trust and respect now give way to fear, disdain and suspicion. Moreover, this perception of fear and disdain is increasingly being translated into social policies that signal the shrinking of democratic public spheres, the hijacking of civic culture, and the increasing militarization of public space. . . . In many suburban malls young people (especially youth of color) cannot even shop or walk around without either appropriate identification cards or in the company of their parents. (p. xvii)

Educators of various races have been led to believe that urban students are incapable of learning and are destined to lives of crime or poverty. The remarks of these Black girls about rap music reveal deeply rooted constructions of racism, classism, essentialism, and White patriarchy that are impeding their natural resistance. Therefore, by refusing to employ critical pedagogy in our classrooms, we choose to fail our Black girls, and all youth, as they consume Black popular culture texts without educators, culturally relevant pedagogy, Hip Hop feminism, and media literacy.

Additionally, and perhaps more important than teaching youth through a culturally relevant pedagogy lens grounded in Hip Hop, is teaching them African American and Latino/a history. Dagbovie (2010) argues that Black history is relevant to the Hip Hop generation. He suggests, "Hip Hop culture is the single most widespread preoccupation among today's African American and African diasporan youth and has the potential to play an important role in rejuvenating the modern black history movement and raising the Hip Hop generation's cultural and historical consciousness" (p. 322). Hip Hop music and culture are a direct reflection of varying experiences of Black and Brown people. This history is rich because marginalized youth of color created a cultural movement rooted in their Black lineage that spoke and still speaks back to Americanism. KRS-One (2003) said it best when auguring the significance of linking Hip Hop to history:

> History inspires. History teaches. History also guides....We, as a Hip Hop people, must come out of the past and into our present. We, as a Hip Hop people, must re-create ourselves. True freedom for us Hiphoppas is to create and live a lifestyle that uniquely empowers us....We Hiphoppas will be busy at work creating a history that simply works better for our children. (p. 145, 154–55)

Retooling students with their history as Hiphoppas is empowering and possible. Our teaching force currently, and over the next ten to twenty years, is young and influenced by Hip Hop, no matter the teachers' race, gender, class or sexuality. Many Black and Brown students who enter into teaching will embody Hip Hop. Therefore, we need school officials to allow teachers to bring themselves and their culture into the classroom, so teachers and students feel culturally affirmed in their learning environments. Howard (2001) argues that one factor contributing to the underachievement of African American students is the "cultural incongruence between African American students and their teachers" (p. 181). Many African American students enter classrooms where the cultural mismatch between them and their teacher is so wide that learning is undermined (Howard, 2001). Pedagogical approaches that center on Hip Hop music and culture can enhance the reading, writing, scientific, and critical thinking skills of urban learners. Such methods may also awaken the rich African and African American spirit that is inside every Black and Brown student simply waiting to be released. However, we must be careful not to romanticize history. Ransby and Matthews (1993) remind us that, "the great African past which we are told we need to recreate is also a patriarchal past in which men and women knew their respective place. These unequal gender roles are then redefined euphemistically as 'complementary' rather than relationships of subordination and domination" (p. 59). This historic conundrum is why feminism must play a role in helping both young men and women critique society. hooks (2000) defines feminism as "a movement to end sexism, sexist exploitation, and oppression" (p. 1). She adds that, "feminists are made, not born" (p. 7). Teaching youth through a Hip Hop feminist perspective is "consciousness-raising" (hooks, 2000, p. 7) and fundamental to revolutionary change. Eradicating patriarchy cannot be achieved without teaching a "[m]ass-based feminist education for critical consciousness" (hooks, 2000, p. 114), embedded within Hip Hop, and projected out to society. We must start to rebrand feminism for a feminist movement within Hip Hop and education. What makes Hip Hop ingenious, uplifting, and therapeutic is that it is rooted in liberation. That is why Hip Hop must be reframed to incorporate feminism, so patriarchy can be challenged, and Hip Hop can begin the process of living up to its full potential. I believe with all my heart and conviction that Hip Hop and feminism can and will inspire our youth because it inspired and transformed me. Let me close by sampling Tupac, because no one has said it better than he: "Hip Hop may not change the world, but I guarantee it will spark the brain that will."

# Regrets

I stated at this book's outset that I did not live with regrets, because Jay-Z informed me that one could not be successful dwelling in the past. I have always taken his words to heart. Therefore, I do not have many regrets in life. However, I regret my research questions pertaining to this study. Going into my dissertation, I thought it was important to understand how Black girls read the text of rap music and culture in relation to their everyday lives. I still think that is an important question, but it is inefficient and ineffectual on its own. In this book's last chapter, I argue that teachers need to engage students in critical and culturally responsive pedagogies, which I believe is true—but what about the responsibility of urban researchers? I entered my dissertation eager to examine the lives of Black girls but only as an observer. I never once considered infusing Hip Hop pedagogy into my research, even knowing its power in and out of the classroom, because as a young researcher I was concerned with research and not the practice of educating. At the time, I did not know the two went hand-in-hand in order for research to be impactful. I remember thinking throughout my study, especially during data collection, that I needed to create a class or a workshop for the girls on media literacy. But time stopped me. Or should I say the fear of time stopped me. I was scared that if I added a media literacy aspect to the study so late into data collection that I would never finish my dissertation. I was apprehensive about restructuring my study because I would have had to alert the university of my changes and resubmit my research proposal. Also, I would have had to get permission from the parents and the community center to conduct workshops with the teens. All of these circumstances—which were not undoable, by any means—derailed me from being a social justice researcher and not just a researcher. Thus, I regret not being more to the girls than a researcher during the time of the study. I regret not empowering them with a structure that would have allowed them to challenge misogyny and heterosexist male fantasies, instead of just narrating them.

I regret entering my dissertation aware of my internalized homophobia and how it has affected me as a researcher. I lost valued time with the girls, which I am still trying to make up to this day, because I feared what they would think of me. My regrets have made me a better person and researcher. I hope anyone reading this book will learn from my mistakes and not be afraid to create change, no matter the research location or circumstances. I will now close with an academic taboo—a quote. Audre Lorde (2007), reflecting on Paulo Freire, writes, "The true focus of revolutionary change is never the oppressive situations which we seek to escape, but that piece of the oppressor which is planted deep within us" (p. 123). Lorde's words resonate more with me now than when I first read them years ago, as I continue my constant effort to fight, confront, and challenge the oppressor that lies deep within me.

# References

Adams, T. M., & Fuller, D. B. (2006). The words have changed but the ideology remains the same: Misogynistic lyrics in rap music. *Journal of Black Studies*, 36(6), 938 - 957.

Akan, G. E., & Grilo. C. M. (1995). Sociocultural influences on eating attitudes and behaviors, body image, and psychological functioning: A comparison of African-American, Asian-American, and Caucasian college women. *International Journal of Eating Disorders 18*, 181–87.

Akinyele. (1996). Put it in your mouth. On *Put it in your mouth.* Stress/Zoo/BMG Records.

Alexander, A. L. (1995). She's no lady, she's a nigger: Abuses, stereotypes, and realities from the middle passage to capital (and Anita) Hill. In A. F. Hill & E. C. Jordan (Eds.), *Race, gender and power in America: The legacy of the Hill-Thomas hearings* (pp. 3–25). New York: Oxford University Press.

Alexander, M. (2010). *The new Jim Crow: Mass incarceration in the age of colorblindness.* New York: New Press.

Alim, S, H. (2004). *You know my steez: An ethnographic and sociolinguistic study of styleshifting in black American speech community*. Durham, NC: Duke University Press.

Arnett, J. J. (2002). The sounds of sex: Sex in teens' music and music videos. In J. D. Brown, J. R. Steele, & K. Walsh-Childers (Eds.), *Sexual teens, sexual media* (pp. 253–264). Mahwah, NJ: Lawrence Erlbaum Associates.

Ashcraft, C. (2006). "Girl, you better go get you a condom": Popular culture and teen sexuality as resources for critical multicultural curriculum. *Teachers College Record, 108*(10), 21–45.

Baldwin, J. (1985). The discovery of what it means to be an American. In *The price of the ticket: Collected nonfiction* (1948–1985). New York: St. Martin's.

Baker, H. A. (1993). *Black Studies, rap, and the academy.* University of Chicago Press.

Bandura, A. (1989). Social cognitive theory. *Annals of Child Development*, 6(1), 1–60.

Banks, J. A. (1993). The canon debate, knowledge construction, and multicultural education. *Educational Researcher, 22*(5), 4–14.

Barlow, W. (1999). *Voice over.* Philadelphia: Temple University Press.

Basu, D. (2005). A critical examination of the political economy of the hip-hop industry. In C. Cecilia, J. Whitehead, P. Mason, & J. Stewart (Eds.), *African Americans in the US economy* (pp. 290–305). Lanham, MD: Rowman and Littlefield.

Bell, D. (1992). *Faces at the bottom of the well.* New York: Basic.

Bem, S. L. (1993) *The lenses of gender: Transforming the debate on sexual inequality*. New Haven, CT: Yale University Press.

Bowleg, L, Craig, M., & Burkholder, G. (2004). Rising and surviving: A conceptual model of active coping among black lesbians. *Cultural Diversity and Ethnic Minority Psychology*, *10*(3), 229–240.

Brown, J. C. (1993). Which black is beautiful? *Advertising Age*, 64(19), 507–511.

Brown, N. R. (2009). *Black girlhood celebration: Toward a hip hop feminist pedagogy.* New York: Peter Lang.

Burbules, N. C., & Berk, R. (1999). Critical thinking and critical pedagogy: Relations, differences, and limits. In T. S. Popkewitz & L. Fendler (Eds.), *Critical theories in education* (pp. 45–65). New York: Routledge. [Also retrieved from http://faculty.Ed.uiuc.edu/burbules/ncb/papers/critical.html on 20 March 2008.]

Bush, J. (2003). *The gold club: The Jacklyn "Diva" Bush story: How I went from gold room to court room.* San Jose, CA: Milligan.

Butler, J. (1990). *Gender trouble: Feminism and the subversion of identity*. New York: Routledge.

Clay, A. (2003). Keepin' it real: Black youth, hip-hop culture, and black identity. *American Behavioral Scientist, 46*(10), 1346.

Clay, A. (2007). "I used to be scared of the dick": Queer women of color, hip-hop, and black masculinity. In G. D. Pough, E. Richardson, A. Durham, and R. Raimist (Eds.), *Home Girls Make Some Noise!: Hip-Hop Feminism Anthology* (pp. 149–165). Monroe, CA: Parker Publishing.

Collins, P. H. (2000). *Black feminist thought : Knowledge, consciousness, and the politics of empowerment* (2nd ed.). New York: Routledge.

Collins, P. H. (2004). *Black sexual politics: African Americans, gender, and the new racism*. New York: Routledge.

Courtwright, J., & Baran, S. (1980). The acquisition of sexual information by young people. *Journalism Quarterly*, 57, 107–114.

Crawford, I., Allison, K., Zamboni, B. D., & Soto, T. (2002). The influence of dual-identity development on the psychological functioning of African-American gay and bisexual men. *Journal of Sex Research, 39(3)*, 179–189.

Creswell, J. W. (2003). *Research design: Qualitative, quantitative, and mixed methods approaches*. Thousand Oaks, CA: Sage Publications Inc.

Cross, W. E., Jr. (1991). *Shades of black: Diversity in African-American identity.* Philadelphia: Temple University Press.

Crouch, S. (2006). Interview with Stanley Crouch. Retrieved June 2, 2008 from http://www.freerepublic.com/focus/f-news/1741532/posts.

Dagbovie, P. G. (2010). "Of all our studies, history is best qualified to reward our research": Black history's relevance to the hip hop generation. In D. Alridge, J. B. Stewart & V. P. Franklin (Eds.), *Message in the music: Hip hop history & pedagogy.* Washington, DC: Association for the Study of African American Life and History.

Denzin, N., & Lincoln, Y. (1994). Introduction: Entering the field of qualitative research. In N. Denzin & Y. Lincoln (Eds.), *Handbook of qualitative research* (pp. 1–17). Thousand Oaks, CA: Sage Publications.

Desai, S. R. (2010). *Emancipate yourself from mental slavery/None but ourselves can free our minds: Spoken word as a site/sight of resistance, reflection and rediscovery* (Unpublished doctoral dissertation). University of California, Los Angeles.

Dewan, S. (March 11, 2006). Gentrification changing face of new Atlanta, *The New York Times*. Retrieved May 18, 2010 from http://www.nytimes.com/2006/03/11/national/11atlanta.html?pagewanted=all.

Dillard, C. (2000). The substance of things hoped for, the evidence of things not seen: Examining an endarkened feminist epistemology in educational research and leadership. *International Journal of Qualitative Studies in Education, 13*(6), 661–681.

Dimitriadis, G. (1999). Hip hop to rap: Some implications of an historically situated approach to performance. *Text and Performance Quarterly*, *19*(4), 355–369.

Dimitriadis, G. (2001). *Performing identity/performing culture: Hip hop as text, pedagogy, and lived practice*: New York: Peter Lang.

Dimitriadis, G. (2003). *Friendship, cliques, and gangs: Young black men coming of age in urban America.* New York: Teachers College Press.

Dionne, P. S., & Phillips, L. D. (2003). Freaks, gold diggers, divas, and dykes: The sociohistorical development of adolescent African American women's sexual scripts. *Sexuality & Culture, 7*(1), 3–49.

DiPlacido, J. (1998). Minority stress among lesbians, gay men, and bisexuals: A consequence of heterosexism, homophobia, and stigmatization. In G. M. Herek (Ed.), *Stigma and sexual orientation: Understanding prejudice against lesbians, gay men, and bisexuals* (pp. 138–159). Thousand Oaks, CA: Sage Publications.

Duggan, L. (2003). *The twilight of equality: Neoliberalism, cultural politics and the attack on democracy.* Boston, MA: Beacon Press.

DuRant, R. H., Rich, M., Emans, S. J., Rome, E. S., Allred, E., & Woods, E. R. (1997). Violence and weapon carrying in music videos. A content analysis. *Pediatrics, 151*(5), 443–448.

Dyson, M. E. (1996). *Race rules: Navigating the color line*. Reading, MA: Addison-Wesley.

Dyson, M. E. (2007). *Know what I mean?: Reflections on hip hop*. New York: Basic Civitas Books.

Dyson, M. E. (2010). One love, two brothers, three verses. In M. E. Dyson & S. Daulatzai (Eds.), *Born to use mics: Reading Nas' illmatic*, (pp. 129–150). New York: Basic Civitas Books.

*Ebony* (December, 2004). Megachurches: Large congregations spread across Black America. Retrieved May 4, 2012, http://books.google.com/books?id=HssGvXb2xeMC&q=mega#v=snippet&q=mega&f=false.

Emdin, C. (2010a). *Urban science education for the hip-hop generation*. New York: Sense Publishers.

Emdin, C. (2010b). Affiliation and alienation: Hip-hop, rap, and urban science education. *Journal of Curriculum Studies*, *42*(1), 1–25.

Emerson, R. A. (2002). "Where my girls at?": Negotiating black womanhood in music videos. *Gender & Society*, *16*(1), 115–135.

Evans-Winters, V. E. (2005). *Teaching black girls: Resiliency in urban classrooms*. New York: Peter Lang Publishing.

Fiasco, L. (2007). Dumb it down. On *the cool*. 1st & 15th, Atlantic.

Fine, M. (1994). Working the hyphens. In N. K. Denzin & Y. S. Lincoln (Eds.), *Handbook of qualitative research*. 2nd ed. (pp. 70–82). Thousand Oaks, CA: Sage Publications.

Fine, M., & Ruglis, J. (2009). Circuits and consequences of dispossession: The racialized realignment of the public sphere for U.S. youth. *Transforming Anthropology*, *17*(1), 20–33.

Fisher, M. T. (2007). *Writing in rhythm: Spoken word poetry in urban classrooms*. New York: Teachers College Press.

Fitts, M. (2008). "Drop it like it's hot": Culture industry laborers and their perspectives on rap music video production. *Meridians*, 8(1), 211–235.

Ford, G. (2002). *Hip-hop and the hard right: Media-made illusions of power.* Retrieved Dec 12, 2007 from http://www.blackcommentator.com/past_issues.html.

Forman, M. & Neal, M. A. (2004). *That's the joint!: The hip-hop studies reader.* New York: Routledge.

Foucault, M. (1995). Strategies of power. In W. Anderson (Ed.), *The truth about the truth: De-confusing and re-constructing the postmodern world* (pp. 40–45). New York: Tarcher/Putnam.

Foucault, M. (1980). *Power/Knowledge: Selected interviews and other writings, 1972–1977.* New York: Pantheon.

Foucault, M. (1977). *Discipline and punish: The birth of the prison.* London: Penguin.

Frank, B. (1987). Hegemonic heterosexual masculinity, *Studies in Political Economy*, Autumn, 159–170.

Freire, P. (1994). *Education for critical consciousness.* New York: Continuum.

Freire, P. (2000). *Pedagogy of the oppressed* (30th anniversary ed.). New York: Continuum.

Gan, S., Zillman, D., & Mitrook, M. (1997). Stereotyping effect of black women's sexual rap on white audiences. *Basic and Applied Social Psychology, 19*, 381–399.

Gaunt, R. (2006). Biological essentialism, gender ideologies, and role attitudes: What determines parents' involvement in child care. *Sex Roles*, 55, 223–233.

Gay, G. (2000). *Culturally responsive teaching: Theory, research, and practice.* New York: Teachers College Press.

George, N. (1999). *Hip hop America.* New York: Penguin.

Gerbner, G., Gross, L., Morgan, M., & Signorelli, N. (1994). Growing up with television: The cultivation perspective. In J. Bryant & D. Zillmann (Eds.),

*Media effects: Advances in theory and research* (pp. 17–41). Hillsdale, NJ: Lawrence Erlbaum Assoc.

Gilroy, P. (1994). *The black Atlantic: Modernity and double consciousness.* Cambridge, MA: Harvard University Press.

Giroux, H. (1988). *Teachers as intellectuals: Toward a critical pedagogy of learning.* Granby, MA: Bergin & Garvey.

Giroux, H. A. (2003). *The abandoned generation: Democracy beyond the culture of fear.* New York: Palgrave Macmillan.

Giroux, H. A. (2006). *America on the edge: Henry Giroux on politics, culture, and education.* New York: Palgrave Macmillan.

Goddard, T. (2009). Reed wins recount. *Teagan Goddard's Political Wire.* Retrieved May 4, 2012, from http://politicalwire.com/archives/2009-campaign/.

Goodall, N. (1994). Depend on myself: T.L.C. and the evolution of Black female rap. *Journal of Negro History 79*: 85–94.

Gow, J. (1999). Rockin', rappin', and religion: Programming strategy on music television. *Popular Music and Society, 23*(2), 17–27.

Gramick, J. (1983). Homophobia: A new challenge. *Social Work, 28*, 137–141.

Graves, K. L. (2009). *And they were wonderful teachers: Florida's purge of gay and lesbian teachers.* Urbana: University of Illinois Press.

Greene, B. (2000). African American lesbian and bisexual women in feminist psychodynamic psychotherapy: Surviving and thriving between a rock and a hard place. In L.C. Jackson & B. Greene (Eds.), *Psychotherapy with African American women: Innovations in psychodynamic perspectives and practice* (pp. 82–125). New York: Guilford Press.

Grem, D. E. (2006). "The south got something to say": Atlanta's dirty south and the southernization of hip-hop America. *Southern Culture, 12*(4), 55–73.

Gruber, E., & Thau, H. (2003). Sexually-related content on television and adolescents of color: Media theory, physiological development, and psychological impact. *Journal of Negro Education, 72*(4), 438–456.

Gurwitt, R. (2008, June 30). Atlanta and the urban future: A major American city has undergone big demographic changes overnight. Will others follow? *Governing: The state and localities.* Retrieved May 4, 2012, from http://www.governing.com/topics/politics/Atlanta-and-the-Urban.html.

Haberman, M. (2000, November). Urban schools: Day camps or custodial centers? *Phi Delta Kappan, 82*(3), 203–208.

Halberstam, J. M. (2005). *In a queer time and place: Transgender bodies, subcultural lives*. New York: New York University Press.

Halberstam, J. (1998). *Masculinity without men: Female masculinity.* Durham, NC: Duke University Press.

Hall, S. (1981). Notes on deconstructing the popular. *People's History and Socialist Theory, 233*, 227–240.

Hall, S. (1983). What is this black in black popular culture. In M. Wallace (Ed.), *Black popular culture.* Boston, MA: Beacon Press.

Hall, S. (1997). *Representation: Cultural representations and signifying practices.* London: Sage Publications.

Halley, J, E. 1993. The construction of heterosexuality. In M. Warner (Ed.), *Fear of a queer planet: Queer politics and social theory* (pp. 82–102). Minneapolis and London: University of Minnesota Press.

Hansen, C. H., & Hansen, R. D. (2000). Music and music videos. In D. Zillmann & P. Vorderer (Eds.), *Media entertainment: The psychology of its appeal* (pp. 175–196). Mahwah, NJ: Lawrence Erlbaum Associates, Inc.

Harbeck, K. (1997). *Gay and lesbian educators: Personal freedoms, public constraints.* Malden, MA: Amethyst.

Hein, V. H. (1972). The image of "a city too busy to hate": Atlanta in the 1960s. *Phylon, 33*(3), 205–221.

Herek, G.M. (2004). Beyond 'homophobia': Thinking about sexual prejudice and stigma in the twenty-first century. *Sexuality Research & Social Policy: A Journal of the NSRC, 1*(2), 6–24.

Hill, M. L. (2009). *Beats, rhymes, and classroom life*. New York: Teachers College Press.

hooks, b. (1992). *Black looks: Race and representation*. Boston, MA: South End Press.

hooks, b. (1994). *Outlaw culture: Resisting representations*. New York: Routledge.

hooks, b. (2000). *Feminism is for everybody: Passionate politics*. Boston, MA: South End Press.

Houston, D. A. (2008). A *dj speaks with hands: Gender education and Hip Hop culture* (Unpublished doctoral dissertation). Ohio University. Doi: UMI3339519.

Howard, T. C. (2001). Powerful pedagogy for African American students: A case of four teachers. *Urban Education, 36*, 179–202.

Hurwitz, J., & Peffley, M. (1997). Public perceptions of race and crime: The role of racial stereotypes. *American Journal of Political Science, 41*(2), 375–401.

Huston, A. C., Wartella, E., & Donnerstein, E. (1998). *Measuring the effects of sexual content in the media*. Menlo Park, CA: Kaiser Family Foundation.

jamila, s. (2002). Can I get a witness? Testimony from a hip-hop feminist. In D. Hernandez & B. Rehman (Eds), *Colonize this! Young women of color on today's feminism* (pp. 382–394). New York: Seal Press.

Jeffries, M. (2007). Re: definitions: The name and the game of hip-hop feminism. In G. D. Pough, E. Richardson, A. Durham, & R. Raimist (Eds.), *Home girls make some noise: Hip hop feminism anthology* (pp. 208–227). Mira Loma, CA: Parker Publishing.

Jennings, K. (1994). *One teacher in 10: Gay and lesbian educators tell their stories*. Los Angeles, CA: Alyson.

Johnson, E. P. (2008). *Sweet tea: Black gay men of the South—An oral history.* Chapel Hill: University of North Carolina Press.

Johnson, L. (1996). Rap, misogyny and racism. *Radical America, 26*, 7–19.

Kelley, R. D. (1998). *Yo' mama's disFunktional!: Fighting the culture wars in urban America.* Boston, MA: Beacon Press.

Kellner, D. (1998). Multiple literacies and critical pedagogy in a multicultural society. *Educational Theory, 48*(1), 103–122.

Kellner, D., & Share, J. (2007). Critical media literacy is not an option. *Learning Inquiry, 1*(1), 59–69.

Keys, C. L. (2004). Empowering self, making choices, creating spaces: Black female identity via rap music performance. In M. Forman & M. A. Neal (Eds.), *That's the joint! Hip-hop studies reader.* New York: Routledge.

Khayatt, M. D. (1992). *Lesbian teachers: An invisible presence.* Albany: State University of New York Press.

Kincheloe, J. L. (2002). *The sign of the burger: McDonald's and the culture of power.* Philadelphia: Temple University Press.

Kincheloe, J. L (2008). *Critical pedagogy primer.* New York: Peter Lang.

Kissen, R. (1996). *The last closet: The real lives of lesbian and gay teachers.* Portsmouth, NH: Heinemann.

Kitwana, B. (2003). *The hip hop generation: Young blacks and the crisis in African American culture.* New York: Basic Civitas Books.

KRS-One. (2003). *Ruminations.* New York: Welcome Rain Publishers.

Kruse, K. M. (2007). *White flight.* Princeton, NJ: Princeton University Press.

Ladson-Billings, G. (1994).*The dreamkeepers: Successful teachers of African American children.* San Francisco: Jossey-Bass.

Ladson-Billings, G., & Tate, W. F. (1995). Toward a critical race theory of education. *Teachers College Record, 97*(1), 47–68.

Lander, C. (2008). *Stuff white people like: A definitive guide to the unique taste of millions.* New York: Random House.

Leard, D. W., & Lashua, B. (2006). Popular media, critical pedagogy, and inner city youth. *Canadian Journal of Education, 29*(1), 244–264.

Lee, C. (1995). The use of signifying as a scaffold for literary interpretation. *Journal of Black Psychology, 21*(4), 357–381.

Lewis, J., & Jhally, S. (1998). The struggle over media literacy. *The Journal of Communication, 48*(1), 109–120.

Lincoln, C. E., & Mamiya, L. H. (1990). *The black church in the African American experience*. Durham, NC: Duke University Press.

Lipsitz, G. (1994). *Dangerous crossroads: Popular music, postmodernism and the poetics of place*. London/New York: Verso.

Loewenstein, S. (1980). Understanding lesbian women. *Social Casework, 61*, 29–38.

Longmore, M. A. 1998. Symbolic interaction and the study of sexuality. *Journal of Sex Research 35*(1), 44–57.

Lorde, A. (2007). *Sister outsider*. Berkeley, CA: Crossing Press.

Love, B. L. (2010). Commercial hip hop: The sounds and images of a racial project. In D. Alridge, J. B. Stewart, & V. P. Franklin (Eds.), *Message in the music: Hip hop, history, and pedagogy* (pp. 55–67). Washington, D.C.: Association for the Study of African American Life and History Press.

Lovejoy, M. (2001). Disturbances in the social body: Differences in body image and eating problems among African American and White women. *Gender and Society, 15*(2), 239–261.

Low, B. (2011). *Slam school: Learning through conflict in the hop-hop and spoken word classroom.* Stanford, CA: Stanford University Press.

Lowry, D. T., Love, G., & Kirby, M. (1981). Sex on the soap operas: Patterns of intimacy. *Journal of Communication, 31*(3), 90–96.

Mahiri, J. (1998). Streets to schools: African American youth culture and the classroom. *Clearing House, 71*(6), 335.

Mahiri, J. (2000). Pop culture pedagogy and the end(s) of school. *Journal of Adolescent & Adult Literacy, 44*(4), 382.

Mahiri, J., & Conner, E. (2003). Black youth violence has a bad rap. *Journal of Social Issues,* 59(1), 121–140.

Margolies, L., Becker, M., & Jackson-Brewer, K. (1987). Internalized homophobia: Identifying and treating the oppressor within. In Boston Lesbian Psychologies Collective (Ed.), *Lesbian psychologies: Explorations and challenges* (pp. 229–241). Urbana, IL: University of Illinois Press.

McBride, J. (2007, April). Hip hop plant. *National Geographic, 211*(4), 100–119.

McLaren, P. (1994). *Life in schools. An introduction to critical pedagogy in the foundations of education.* Chicago: Addison-Wesley.

McLaren, P. (1995). *Critical pedagogy and predatory culture: Oppositional politics in a postmodern era.* New York: Routledge.

McWhorter, J. H. (2003). What's holding blacks back?. City *Journal, 2*(1), 24–32.

Merriam, S. B. (1998). *Qualitative research and case study applications in education.* San Francisco: Jossey-Bass Publishers.

Meyer, I. H. (1995). Minority stress and mental health in gay men. *Journal of Health and Social Behavior, 36*(1), 38–56.

Meyer, I. H. & Dean, L. (1998). Internalized homophobia, intimacy, and sexual behavior among gay and bisexual men. In G.M. Herek (Ed.), *Stigma and sexual orientation: Understanding prejudice against lesbians, gay men, and bisexuals* (pp. 160–186). Thousand Oaks, CA: Sage Publications.

Meyers, M. (2004). African American women and violence: Gender, race and class in the news. *Critical Studies in Mass Communication, 21*(2), 95–118.

Miller, J. (2008). *Getting played: African American girls, urban inequality, and gendered violence.* New York: New York University Press.

Miller-Young, M. (2008). Hip-hop honeys and da hustlaz: Black sexualities in the new hip-hop pornography. *Meridians,* 8(1), 261–292.

Milner, R. (2007). Race, culture, and researcher positionality: Working through dangers seen, unseen, and unforeseen. *Educational Researcher,* 36(7), 388–400.

Morgan. J. (1999). *When chickenheads come home to roost: A hip-hop feminist breaks it down*. New York: Simon & Schuster.

Morrell, E., & Duncan-Andrade, J. M. R. (2002). Promoting academic literacy with urban youth through engaging hip-hop culture. *English Journal, 91*(6), 88–92.

Neal, M. A. (1997). Sold out on soul: The corporate annexation of black popular music. *Popular Music and Society, 21*(3) 117–135.

Neisen, J. H. (1993). Healing from cultural victimization: Recovery from shame due to heterosexism. *Journal of Gay & Lesbian Psychotherapy*, *2*(1), 49–63.

Noguera, P. A. (2008). *The trouble with Black boys and other reflections on race, equity and the future of public education.* New York: Wiley.

Okazawa-Rey, M., Robinson, T., and Ward, J. V. (1987). Black women and the politics of skin color and hair. *Women's Studies Quarterly* 14,13–14.

Oliver, M. B. (1994). Portrayals of crime, race, and aggression in reality-based police shows: A content analysis. *HeinOnline*, 38, 179.

Oliver, M. L., & Shapiro T. M. (1997). *Black wealth/white wealth: A new perspective on racial inequality*. New York: Routledge.

Omi, M., & Winant, H. (1994). *Racial formation in the United States: From the 1960s to the 1980s*. New York: Routledge.

Outkast. (1994). Git up, git out. *Southernplayalisticadillacmuzik*. LaFace Records.

Padesky, C. A. (1988). Attaining and maintaining positive lesbian self-identity: A cognitive therapy approach. *Women & Therapy*, 8(1/2), 145–156.

Palmer, T. (2005). *Country fried soul: Adventures in dirty South hip hop.* San Francisco, CA: Backbeat Books.

Parker, S., Nichter, M., Vuckovic, C. S., & Ritenbaugh, C. (1995). Body image and weight concerns among African-American and white adolescent females: Differences that make a difference. *Human Organization 54*, 103–14.

Peoples, W. A. (2008). "Under construction": Identifying foundations of hip-hop feminism and exploring bridges between black second-wave and hip-hop feminism. *Meridians*, 8(1), 19–52.

Perkins, W. E. (1996). *Droppin' science: Critical essays on rap music and hip hop culture.* Philadelphia, PA: Temple University Press.

Petchauer, E. (2009). Framing and reviewing hip-hop educational research. *Review of Educational Research, (79)*2, 946-978.

Pharr, S. (1988). *Homophobia: A weapon of sexism.* Berkeley, CA: Chardon Press.

Phillips, L. (2006). *The womanist reader*: New York: Routledge.

Plies. (2007). Shawty. On *The real testament.* Big Gates/Slip-n-Slide Records.

Pough, G. D. (2004). *Check it while I wreak it: Black womanhood, hip-hop culture, and the public sphere.* Boston, MA: Northeastern University Press.

Pough, G. (2002). Love feminism but where's my hip-hop? Shaping a black feminist identity. In *Colonize this! Young women of color on today's feminism,* (Eds.), edited by D. Hernandez and B. Rehman, pp. 85–95. New York: Seal Press.

Pruett, K., & Pruett, M. (2009). *Partnership parenting: How men and women parent differently—why it helps your kids and can strengthen your marriage.* New York: Da Capo Lifelong books.

Quinn, T., & Meiners, E. (2009). *Flaunt it!: Queers organizing for public education and justice.* New York: Peter Lang.

Ransby, B. & Matthews, T. (1993). Black popular culture and the transcendence of patriarchial illusions. *Race and Class 34*(1), 57–68.

Richardson, E. (2007). 'She was workin like forreal': Critical literacy and discourse and practices of African American females in the age of hip hop. *Discourse & Society, 18,* 789–809.

Ridout, V., Lauricella, A., & Wartella, E. (2011). *Children, media and race. Media use among White, Black, Hispanic, and Asian American children.* Evanston, IL: Northwestern University .

Roberts, R. (1991). Music videos, performance and resistance: Feminist rappers. *Journal of Popular Culture* 25, 141–42.

Roberts, R. (1994). Ladies first: Queen Latifah's Afrocentric feminist music video. *African American Review* 28, 245–67.

Robinson, E. (2010). Eddie Long isn't practicing what he preaches. *Washington Post*. Retrieved May 19, 2011, from http://www.washingtonpost.com/wpdyn/content/article/2010/09/27/AR2010092704679.html.

Robinson, R. (2010). Harms of anti-gay rhetoric lost as media fixates on Bishop Eddie Long scandal. *Huffington Post.* Retrieved May 20, 2011, from http://www.huffingtonpost.com/rashad-robinson/harms-ofantigayrhetoric_b_750922.html.

Rodriguez, N., & Pinar, W. (Eds). (2007). *Queering straight teachers: Discourse and identity in education.* New York: Peter Lang.

The Roots. (1999). Act Too (The love of my life). On *Things fall apart*. MCA.

Rose, T. (2008). *The hip hop wars*. New York: Basic Civitas Books.

Rose, T. (1991). "Fear of a black planet": Rap music and black cultural politics in the 1990s. *Journal of Negro Education,* 60(3), 276–290.

Rose, T. (1994). *Black noise: Rap music and black culture in contemporary America.* Hanover, NH, and London: Wesleyan University Press.

Ross, M. W., & Rosser, B. R. (1996). Measurement and correlates of internalized homophobia: Factor analytic study. *Journal of Clinical Psychology, 52*, 15–21.

Russell, S. T. (2008). Remembering Lawrence King: An agenda for educators, schools, and scholars. *Teachers College Record*. Retrieved May 9, 2011, from http://www.tcrecord.org/Content.asp?ContentID=15236.

Rutheiser, C. (1996). *Imagineering Atlanta*. New York: Verso Books.

Sarig, R. (2007) *Third coast: OutKast, Timbaland, and how hip hop became a southern thing.* Cambridge, MA: Da Capo Press.

Sears, I. (1991). *Growing up* gay *in the south.* New York: Harrington Press.

Sears, J. T. (2002). The institutional climate for lesbian, gay and bisexual education faculty: What is the pivotal frame of reference? *Journal of Homosexuality, 43*(1), 11–37.

Shapiro, T. M. (2004). *The hidden cost of being African American: How wealth perpetuates inequality.* Oxford, UK: Oxford University Press.

Sharpley-Whiting, T. D. (2007). *Pimps up, ho's down: Hip hop's hold on young black women*. New York: New York University Press.

Shidlo, A. (1994). Internalized homophobia: Conceptual and empirical issues in measurement. In G. M. Herek (Ed.), *Lesbian and Gay Psychology: Theory, Research and Clinical Application* (pp. 176–205). Thousand Oaks, CA: Sage Publications.

Shor, I. (1987). *Critical teaching and everyday life*. Chicago: University of Chicago Press.

Sophie, J. (1987). Internalised homophobia and lesbian identity. *Journal of Homosexuality, 14*, 53–66.

Steele, J. R., & Brown, J. D. (1995). Adolescent room culture: Studying media in the context of everyday life. *Journal of Youth and Adolescence, 24*(5), 551–576.

Steinberg, S. R. (2007). Hollywood's curriculum of Arabs and Muslims in two acts. In. D. Macedo & S. R. Steinberg (Eds.), *Media literacy: A reader* (pp. 299–315). New York: Peter Lang.

Stephens, D., & Few, A. (2007a). Hip hop honey or video ho: African American preadolescents' understanding of female sexual scripts in hip hop culture. *Sexuality & Culture, 11*(4), 48–69.

Stephens, D., & Few, A. (2007b). The effects of images of African American women in hip hop on early adolescents' attitudes toward physical attractiveness and interpersonal relationships. *Sex Roles, 56*(3), 251–264.

Stephens, D. P., & Phillips, L. (2005). Integrating black feminist thought into conceptual frameworks of African American adolescent women's sexual scripting processes. *Sexualities, Evolution & Gender, 7*(1), 3–49.

Storey, J. (1998). *An introduction to cultural theory and popular culture.* Athens, GA: University of Georgia Press.

Story, F. (February, 2007). Built Ford tough. *King.* Retrieved May 4, 2012, from http://www.king-mag.com/04july-aug/covergirl/ford.html

Stovall, D. (2006). We can relate: Hip-hop culture, critical pedagogy, and the secondary classroom. *Urban Education, 41*(6), 585.

Suggs, E., & Srirgus, E. (2009, December 9). Reed in, Norwood concedes. New dawn for Atlanta. *Atlanta Journal Constitution.* Retrieved May 4, 2012, from http://www.ajc.com/news/atlanta/reed-in-norwood-concedes-234950.html.

Sumara, D., & Davis, B. (1999). Interrupting heteronormativity: Toward a queer curriculum theory. *Curriculum Inquiry, 2*, 91–208.

Szymanski, D. M., & Chung, Y. B. (2001). The lesbian internalized homophobia scale: A rational/theoretical approach. *Journal of Homosexuality, 41*(2), 37–52.

Thompson, K. A. (2007). Performing visibility: Freaknic and the spatial politics of sexuality, race, and class in Atlanta. *The Drama Review. 51*(4), 24–46.

Tillman, L. C. (2002). Culturally sensitive research approaches: An African-American perspective. *Educational Researcher, 31*(9), 3.

Torres, M. N., & Mercado, M. D. (2007). The need for critical media literacy in teacher education. In D. Macedo & S. R. Steinberg (Eds.), *Media literacy: A reader* (pp. 537–558). New York: Peter Lang.

Tyler, F. B. (1978). Individual psychosocial competence: A personality configuration. *Educational and Psychological Measurement, 38*, 309–323.

Tyson, C. (1998). A response to "Coloring epistemologies: Are our qualitative research epistemologies racially biased?" *Educational Researcher, 27*(9), 21–22.

Viola, M. (2003). Hip-hop and critical revolutionary pedagogy: Blue scholarship to challenge "The miseducation of the Filipino." *Journal for Critical Education Policy Studies 1*(1). Retrieved June 2, 2008 from http://www.jceps.com/?pageID=article&articleID=71%3E.

Walker, A. (1983). *In search of our mothers' gardens: Womanist prose.* San Diego: Harcourt Brace Jovanovich.

Walker, R. (1995). *To be real: Telling the truth and changing the face of feminism.* New York: Anchor Books.

Ward, E. G. (2005). Homophobia, hypermasculinity, and the US black church. *Culture, Health, and Sexuality, 7*(5), 493–504.

Ward, L. M. (2004). Wading through the stereotypes: Positive and negative associations between media use and black adolescents' conceptions of self. *Developmental Psychology, 40*(2), 284–294.

Ward, L. M., Hansbrough, E., & Walker, E. (2005). Contributions of music video exposure to Black adolescents' gender and sexual schemas. *Journal of Adolescent Research, 20*(2), 143.

Ward, L. M., & Rivadeneyra, R. (1999). Contributions of entertainment television to adolescents' sexual attitudes and expectations: The role of viewing amount versus viewer involvement. *The Journal of Sex Research, 36*(3), 237–249.

Warner, M. (1993). Introduction. In Michael Warner (Ed.), *Fear of a queer planet: Queer politics and social theory*, (pp. vii–xxxi). Minneapolis and London: University of Minnesota Press.

West, C. (2001). *Race matters*. Boston, MA: Beacon Press.

Wheeler, S. C., & Petty, R. E. (2001). The effects of stereotype activation on behavior: A review of possible mechanisms. *Psychology Bulletin, 127*(6), 797–826.

Williams Institute. (2010). The Census Snapshot. Retrieved May 23, 2011, from http://2010.census.gov/partners/pdf/factSheet_General_LGBT.pdf.

Wingood, G. M., DiClemente, R. J., Bernhardt, J. M., Harrington, K., Davies, S. L., Robillard, A., et al. (2003). A prospective study of exposure to rap music videos and African American female adolescents' health. *American Journal of Public Health*, *93*(3), 437–439.

Wise, T. (2009). *Between Barack and a hard place: Racism and white denial in the age of Obama*. San Francisco: City Lights Books.

Ying Yang Twins (2005). Wait (The whisper song). On *United State of Atlanta.* TVT Records.

Zinn, H. (2005). *A people's history of the United States: 1492–present*. New York: Harper Perennial Modern Classics.

# Index

Y

## Studies in the Postmodern Theory of Education

*General Editor*
*Shirley R. Steinberg*

Counterpoints publishes the most compelling and imaginative books being written in education today. Grounded on the theoretical advances in criticalism, feminism, and postmodernism in the last two decades of the twentieth century, Counterpoints engages the meaning of these innovations in various forms of educational expression. Committed to the proposition that theoretical literature should be accessible to a variety of audiences, the series insists that its authors avoid esoteric and jargonistic languages that transform educational scholarship into an elite discourse for the initiated. Scholarly work matters only to the degree it affects consciousness and practice at multiple sites. Counterpoints' editorial policy is based on these principles and the ability of scholars to break new ground, to open new conversations, to go where educators have never gone before.

For additional information about this series or for the submission of manuscripts, please contact:

Shirley R. Steinberg
c/o Peter Lang Publishing, Inc.
29 Broadway, 18th floor
New York, New York 10006